RADICAL POLITICS IN MEGHALAYA

RADICAL POLITICS IN MEGHALAYA
Problems and Prospects

Susmita Sen Gupta

KALPAZ

Radical Politics in Meghalaya—Problems and Prospects

ISBN: 978-81-7835-742-3

Published in 2009 in India by
Kalpaz Publications
C-30, Satyawati Nagar,
Delhi-110052
E-mail: kalpaz@hotmail.com
Phone : 9212729499

Lasser Type Setting by: Quick Media, Delhi
Printed at : Singhal Print Media, Delhi

Contents

Preface 7

Acknowledgements 11

1. Radical Politics in North East India : Origin and Development of CPI 13

2. Demand of the Hill State and the Role of the CPI 63

3. Front Organizations of the CPI in Meghalaya 95

4. Meghalaya CPI and State Assembly Elections—An Assessment 133

5. Conclusion 183

Appendices 201

Bibliography 229

Index 237

Preface

The most significant agent of radical politics in Meghalaya is the CPI which is one of the oldest political parties in the country. According to declarations issued by its highest national organization, it strives to achieve the establishment of national democracy and create conditions for advancing to the goal of establishment of socialism by peaceful means. The working class and their allies will strive their utmost to overcome the resistance of the forces of reaction and transform Parliament from an instrument serving the bourgeoisie into a genuine instrument of the people's will for effecting the fundamental transformation in the economic, social and State structure.

Thus, it appears that the CPI is a progressive party interested in the welfare of the people. The national party has a branch in Meghalaya which was originally a part of Assam CPI. After the formation of Meghalaya on January 21, 1972, the Meghalaya unit of the CPI was born. The CPI was the first national party to welcome and support the formation of Meghalaya as an Autonomous State. From its very inception, the CPI claims to have championed the cause of the tribal people and stood for safeguarding their identity. As part of its All-India Programme, the

CPI in Meghalaya seeks the introduction of radical agrarian reform in the State. The party is of the opinion that compulsory universal primary education, agrarian reform and rapid industrialization would pave the way for educational, cultural and economic development of the State. The CPI appeals to the farmers and the rural poor to fight against exploitation and unjust practices to bring about a better system. It seeks to preserve the unity and integrity of the people by fighting against communal and chauvinist forces.

Thus, it appears that the CPI has a concrete political programme for the solution of the burning problems of Meghalaya. The party projects itself as the true promoter of Meghalayan interests. Nevertheless, the CPI has not been able to make any significant breakthrough in the politics of Meghalaya. The CPI has contested all the assembly elections held in Meghalaya so far without achieving any success. This gives rise to a number of questions. What is the relevance of the CPI in the Meghalayan situation? What are the oddities faced by it in its activities in Meghalaya? And so on. The leaders of the party in Meghalaya appear to hold the view that the CPI has failed to achieve any significant political gains in Meghalaya because of the fear among the tribal people that Communists do not allow people to worship God in their own ways. The question is whether this opinion is based on facts. It will also be interesting to examine the manner in which the CPI works at the grass-roots level in Meghalaya. This will, of course, necessitate an enquiry into the working of the various front organizations of the party. As the book proceeds, the following questions are proposed to be investigated :

1. Does the perspective adopted by the CPI postulate an understanding of the political situation of Meghalaya?
2. What are the main impediments faced by the CPI in Meghalaya in pursuing its radical politics?
3. What is the nature of its front organizations?
4. What are the reasons for the failure of the CPI in Meghalaya elections?

An investigation on the above lines should enable us to understand the reasons behind the failure of radical politics in Meghalaya and to examine whether such politics has any future prospects in the State.

Shillong **Susmita Sen Gupta**

Acknowledgements

I wish to express my deep and sincere gratitude to Prof. A.K. Baruah, of the Department of Political Science, North-Eastern Hill University, whose personal involvement and sustained inspiration have been indispensable for the completion of the book. I would also like to express my gratitude to all my teachers and colleagues in the Department for their valuable suggestions from time to time.

I am specially thankful to the veteran Communist leader and Editor of the *Shillong Observer,* Shri Prafulla Misra, and Shri Benubinode Chaudhury who not only provided me with relevant research materials on the Communist Party at their disposal, but also frankly expressed their views on the problems and prospects of the party in North East India as a whole. I also express my deep sense of indebtedness to Late Shri Binoy Lahiri, Shri Ranjit Kar, Shri Umapada Deb, Shri M. Chakravarty, Mr. Robin Rema and Mr. Dalington Dympep who gave me valuable information on the front organizations of the Communist Party in Meghalaya and on the nature of various electoral constituencies from which the party contested. I shall be failing in my duty if I do not mention the assistance I procured from the Gauhati Office of the Assam State Council of the CPI.

I would like to put on record the ever-willing assistance extended to me in various ways by my friends, Sutapa and Uttama. The encouragement and inspiration given to me by my parents is deeply appreciated and I remain indebted to them.

I take this opportunity to put on record my thanks to Ms. M. Warbah for her competent and flawless typing of the manuscript.

Shillong **Susmita Sen Gupta**

1

Radical Politics in North East India : Origin and Development of the CPI

The history of Indian contacts with the International Communist Movement and the formation of the Communist Party of India abroad reaches back into the exciting days of World War I when a section of militant nationalists realized the naivete and futility of sporadic terrorism and felt that it was only with external assistance that an organized national revolutionary movement could be brought about and the country's independence won.[1] Drawing inspiration from the events in the USSR and being convinced that liberation could be achieved only through a communist movement, some Indian nationalists[2] formed the Communist Party of India at Tashkent in 1921.[3] According to Rafiq Ahmad, one of the Muhajirs who set out for Tashkent, "As a matter of fact, the Communist Party of India had been set up towards the end of 1920 at Tashkent... ."[4]

There appears to be some controversy about the exact place, date and situation of the formation of the CPI. But since this emigre Communist Party of India was affiliated to the Communist International in the first half of 1921, Muzaffar Ahmad concludes that "the date of the Party's foundation, if it was not 1920, could not have been later than early 1921".[5] It may be noted here that Rafiq Ahmad's account of the formation of the CPI has been corroborated by Evelyne, wife of M. N. Roy. Jane Degras quotes her as saying that the CPI was founded in October, 1920.[6]

In India, a movement was already afoot for the formation of a Communist Party of India as a result of which a number of amorphous groups were operating in different parts of the country. Of the Communist groups that lay scattered around the country, most active were those in Bombay, Calcutta, Madras, Lahore and Kanpur.[7] The First Indian Communist Conference was held on December 26, 1925, at Kanpur. Despite sharp differences of opinion over the ideological orientation of the party, a Central Committee was formed bringing together the representatives of the early Communist groups formed in Calcutta, Bombay, Madras, Punjab and the North in general. The first Constitution of the Communist Party of India was published towards the end of 1926. The newly constituted Central Committee of the Communist Party of India met in several secret sessions during 1926 and 1929 to work out a programme of action for the organization of Communist movement in India.[8] In 1930, the Party was formally affiliated to the Communist International.[9]

The leadership of the Communist Party of India when it was united on 18 August 1959, decided to adopt the date of the Kanpur Communist Conference as the date of the formation of the party, but we cannot minimize the importance and significance of the foundation of the party at Tashkent in October 1920.[10] On the basis of the CPI formed in Tashkent, a Centre was created abroad which did a lot of ideological and propaganda work. It was indeed a two-way process in which the independent thinking and acting of groups and comrades here played a considerable part.[11]

Just after a year of its formation, in the Gauhati session of the Indian National Congress held in 1926, the CPI released a manifesto calling for complete independence and stressing the need for building up organization of workers and peasants on class basis. These aims were spelt out at the Political Sufferers' Conference held during the Gauhati Session and presided over by Dr. Bhupendranath Dutta.[12] The formation and growth of a Communist Party presupposes a certain degree of political consciousness of the working class. In Assam also, the formal establishment of the State unit of the CPI was preceded by more than a decade of preparatory work to awaken the working people to a consciousness of the social conditions in which they lived. The October Revolution inspired a large number of Assamese intellectuals in the twenties and thirties. Despite the limitations of their ideas and information regarding the developments in

Soviet Russia, they all welcomed the changes ushered in by the Socialist Revolution.[13]

Communist activity in India was abruptly cut short by the arrest under instructions of the British Government in India of thirty-one of its most important leaders from different parts of the country on 20th March 1929. The arrests were accompanied by comprehensive search operations throughout the country. From the documents which became available for open investigation after the searches, the duties and tasks of the Communist Party of India as enjoined from time to time by the Comintern were for the first time brought into day light.[14] The trial that was organized against the Communists on the basis of these findings became known as the Meerut Conspiracy case. It made martyrs out of the communists and gave them a unique niche in Indian political life. The trial evoked widespread nationalist sympathy for the accused at Meerut.[15] This case had its impact on the students of Assam, too. Young Jagannath Bhattacharya, the first Communist of Assam, who was then a student of the Banaras Hindu University, was deeply moved. Jadu Saikia, an Assamese Law student of Banaras Hindu University in 1936, states while trying to recollect his memories that he was deeply moved by the Meerut Trial and came into contact with the communists and socialists in Banaras. Saikia distributed both legal and illegal socialist and communist literature among the left-wingers of the Congress in Assam. Saikia mentions that Dhiren

Dutta who had contacts with the Dacca and Calcutta Communists brought banned literature into Assam.[16] Bishnu Borah, a veteran communist leader, says that during that period, Shillong became the centre of smuggling of banned Marxist literature from Sylhet into the Brahmaputra Valley.[17]

The political awakening among the students in Assam in the 1920s caused alarm to the British rulers who sought to counteract it with various measures. Mr. Cunningham, the then D.P.I. of Assam, issued a circular in May 1929, banning participation of students in political activities. Refusing to comply with the circular, many students left the institutions. Within a few months, a number of Swadeshi educational institutions sprang up throughout Assam which in course of time became centres of political movement of students. The Civil Disobedience Movement in Assam initially took the form of a student agitation against the Cunningham Circular.[18] From amongst the students and youth who were imprisoned or expelled from educational institutions, quite a few became the future cadres of Terrorist movement and later of Communist movement.[19]

The Gandhi-Irwin Pact was signed on March 5, 1931, leading to disillusionment among the youth of Assam. These sections, particularly those from the urban areas of Surma Valley constituted revolutionary groups. Ultimately, most of these groups merged into 'Tarun Sangha'. The formation of the Sangha was followed by several mail robberies, including the Tinsukia Mail Robbery, robberies in the houses of moneylenders and action against police personnel responsible for the torturing of Satyagrahis.[20] Some of the leaders of Tarun Sangha accepted scientific socialism on being encouraged by their erstwhile Calcutta colleagues who had already given up terrorism and adopted scientific socialism. These groups remained inside the National Congress and some of them held important offices in the Congress and later in the Congress Socialist Party.[21]

By 1938, Congress Socialist Party groups were functioning in several sub-divisions of Assam, such as Golaghat, Dibrugarh, Sylhet and Goalpara. Leaders of these groups conferred together and decided to take steps towards forming the Assam Congress Socialist Party. Biswanath Mukherjee, Joint Secretary of the All India Students Federation (AISF), while on a tour of Assam in 1938, had established contacts with them and suggested such a move.[22] On September 30, 1939, a provincial conference was held in Golaghat which was presided over by Somnath Lahiri, a veteran communist leader and pioneer of the trade union movement. The Assam Congress Samajtantri Dal (Assam Congress Socialist Party) was born as a result of the Conference with Sriman Prafulla Goswami as General Secretary of the 21 member Executive Committee. On the same night, a more exclusive inner group was formed to carry on secret communist activities. On 20 April 1940, the Executive Committee of the Assam CSP held its first meeting at the house of Siblal Pandit at Lumding.[23]

Pro-Communist students seemed to have been playing an important role in the politics of Assam. In 1939, a conference of Assam Chhatra Sanmilan was held at Jorhat.[24] It was presided over by Prof. Humayun Kabir and addressed by Mansur Habib, a prominent Communist leader of Bengal and Biswanath Mukherjee, Joint Secretary of AISF. The Conference decided to affiliate the Chhatra Sanmilan to AISF. Gaurisankar Bhattacharya was elected General Secretary of Assam Chhatra Sanmilan and Dadhi Mahanta editor of its organ, *Milan.* Amiya Dasgupta, the AISF leader, remained in Assam for purposes of organization until he was externed from the province in June 1940. He had been deputed by the Bengal Committee of the CPI to organize a communist group in the Brahmaputra Valley under the cover of the CSP. He helped radicalization of the Students' Federation and formation of Marxist Study Circles in several towns of Brahmaputra Valley.[25] Influence of the communists on the Assam students was thus increasing steadily.

A Joint Conference of the Students' Federation bodies of both the Valleys, Brahmaputra and Barak as well as of Manipur and the Hills, was held at Shillong in the middle of 1940 with Humayun Kabir in the chair. The conference elected Gaurisankar Bhattacharya as President and Pranesh Chandra

Biswas as Secretary of the emergent confederation. The Conference passed resolutions condemning the Defence of India Rules and directing students not to render any assistance to war efforts. Biswas and Anjali Das, and later Bishnu Bora, went out on an organizational tour of Assam districts, carrying on anti-war propaganda.[26] Tea garden workers of Assam went on a strike in protest against the compulsory recruitment of labour for war efforts. Students supported the workers. On 6th December, 1941, the Deputy Commissioner of Kamrup, Humphrey, ordered lathi and bayonet charge on anti-war exhibition demonstration of Gauhati students resulting in severe injuries to a large number of them. This occasioned a province-wise continuous student strike and a wave of protest hartals. At the initiative of the AISF, a 'Gauhati Day' was observed for anti-war demonstrations all over the country.[27] This protest movement contributed in a big way to the growth of anti-imperialist militant student movement in general and Students' Federation in particular. Assam Provincial Students' Federation led by the Revolutionary Communist Party of India (R.C.P.I.) students who took active part in the 6th December demonstration also consolidated its own base.[28] During this period, girl students' committees associated with the Students' Federation were also formed in several towns.

Banned during the years 1934-July 1942, the Communist Party of India carried on its underground activities under the cover of mass organizations. Hence the influence of the Communists was increasing steadily irrespective of the ban.

When Germany declared was against the Soviet Union on June 22, 1941, the Communists characterized the war as "people's war". This stand led to controversy in the political circles of India at that time.[29] The communist decision to support the war resulted in the gradual release by the British administration in India of the communist leaders from detention and on 24th July 1942, to the lifting of the ban on the Communist Party itself. In Assam, Biresh Misra, a leader of the Sylhet District Congress Committee (and also a communist), who was in jail since 1940, was released in time for participation in the first legal meeting of the CPI at Sylhet on 27 July 1942.[30]

The new CPI line was first pushed among the students through the platform of the Assam Chhatra Sanmilan. With some difficulties and despite an organizational split in May 1942, it continued to retain substantial influence over the student community.[31] In fact, the All India Students' Federation was already split into two rival bodies in 1940. In Assam, one of the rival bodies was represented by the CPI-led Assam Chhatra Sanmilan and the other by the RCPI-led Assam Provincial Students' Federation.[32] Communists held key offices in the District Congress Committee of Sylhet and Cachar and were thus able to keep these committees somewhat in restraint in course of the August turmoil.[33]

Communist activities in North Eastern India thus continued to spread. The trial of INA officers by the British in November 1945, gave vent to an unprecedented upsurge of protest demonstrations all over India. Solidarity actions in the wake of all these events of national importance were organized by student organizations and workers' trade unions led by the Assam communists in Shillong, Gauhati, Tezpur and other towns.[34] It was in the course of such political activities that the CPI in Assam was able to restore its patriotic image that had been damaged after 1942 following its pro-war stand.[35]

CPI in North-East India and Trade Union Movement

The emancipation of the working class from the exploitation of the employers and improvement of the overall working conditions and wage standards being the cherished goals of the Communist ideology, the CPIs role in the trade union movement of India in general and of Assam in particular assumes special significance. As a spearhead of left-wing political movement, modern trade unionism came to India after the close of World War I when to the piquant political situation of the country had been added a number of serious socio-economic problems. On the economic front, the post-war years witnessed an unprecedented crisis resulting in the worsening conditions of life and work of the Indian workers.[36]

In Assam, the persistent economic depression of the 1930s had hit hard not only the agriculturists, but also the province's trade and industries. Planters and industrialists naturally tried to shift the burden onto workers' shoulders. The latter, of course, resisted. On the peasants front, too, old style Ryot Sabhas were giving way, here and there, to militant Kisan Sabhas (or Samitis) of a new type.[37] The socialist and communist ideology began to play a significant role in organizing students, workers and peasants on a radical platform.

Now, although trade unionism in India as an organized movement was, to a large extent, due to the impact of socialist ideas, the force of that impact was sought to be modified by the moderate attitude of the nationalist leaders who were committed to an ideology which was more Fabian than Marxian. Socialism though their professed goal was, there was nothing communist about it.[38] However, due to a decline in the political tempo and demoralization among industrial workers following the great strike wave of 1918-22, the communists intensified their activities to enlist a broad spectrum of working class support for their revolutionary cause and to develop their organizational apparatus within the trade unions.[39] According to Overstreet and Windmiller,[40] it was after the arrival of George Allison (a British Communist) in India in April 1926, that the communists began to "ginger up" their activity in the trade union movement.

During the post-war years, the struggle of the Indian working class suddenly leapt to a position of remarkable strength and trade unionism entered on a period of vigorous growth.[41] Work in the factories and industries in India was jeopardized following several strikes during 1918-22. In Assam, too, a number of strikes paralyzed work in tea gardens, railways and oil companies.[42] All these strikes were, however, unorganized and spontaneous.

In Assam, the railway workers of the Dibrugarh District were organized for the first time on a class basis by Dr. Benoybhusan Chakrabarty, Kedarnath Goswami and Nilmoni Barthakur - Congressmen with sympathies for Socialist and Communist ideology.[43] In the mid 1930s, the workers of the Dibru-Sadia Railway, the Margherita-Ledo Collieries and the A.R.T. owned tea-gardens in Ledo were organized under the Red Flag.[44]

Short-lived strikes in tea-gardens and "a good deal of trouble among railwaymen and contractors' labour, working for the British owned Assam Railways and Trading Company, took place in 1938-39".[45] The annual conference of the A.R. and T. Co. Labour Union was held in March 1942, at Dibrugarh, with Jadunath Saikia in the chair. Under the Communist guidance, the first conference of the Assam Provincial Trade Union Congress was also held at Dibrugarh on 28 November, 1943. On the one hand, it called upon the workers to boost war efforts through increased production and on the other, urged the Government to release the national leaders. The general progress of trade unionism under the banner of the C.P.I. was bound to be slow with its pro-war policy, although such a policy did help to circumvent the lack of civil liberties. The provincial branch of the All India Trade Union Congress (AITUC) held its second annual conference at Gauhati on 26-27 May, 1945. Assam's only central working class organization till then, it continued to be under the Communist domination.[46]

The CPI, therefore, wanted to contest all the four tea-labour seats in Assam in the 1946 elections with necessary Congress support, or at least connivance, which was not forthcoming. Finally, it contested three labour seats on its own strength and was miserably defeated. It also contested and lost three general seats.[47]

The discussion on trade unionism in Assam will be incomplete unless we mention the historic Digboi strike of 1939. The smouldering unrest at the little oil town of Digboi in Lakhimpur District was of great significance as its 10,000 workers were concentrated in a sensitive industrial and plantation area. The Administrative Report for the year 1937-38 did not fail to note the signs of trouble brewing there.[48] A general meeting of the workers of the Assam Oil Company was held on 22 February, 1938, as a consequence of which the A.O.C. Labour Union was formed.[49] The A.O.C. Labour Union, under the Red Flag, became very popular among the workers. Apart from the company employees and contract labour, even the fourth grade employees of Oil Company 'Sahibs' came under its banner. The union submitted a 12-point charter of demands as well as a 14-day strike notice. The Company moved the Government for reconciliation. Meanwhile, the Congress Coalition Ministry led by Gopinath Bordoloi was formed in Assam. But the Congress Ministry failed to extend any protection to the workers. The workers resorted to a strike from April 3, 1939. The course of events took a violent turn when on the night of 18th April, the police shot dead two workers and seriously injured two others who later succumbed to death. This event had its repercussions throughout the province. The failure of the Bordoloi Ministry to offer protection to the workers against the exploitation of the British Oil Company might have brought disillusionment to the younger generation and made them thoroughly cynical about the Congress leadership.[50] The organization of the Digboi labourers as a united force was therefore followed by the youth in Assam turning to progressive ideas.[51] When Digboi-Tinsukia area was declared "protected area" under D.I.R. on September 14, 1939, most of the strike leaders were dubbed communists and were either arrested or externed from Assam, and the workers were subjected to inhuman repression. The historic struggle of the Digboi workers thus came to an end.[52]

The Digboi strike contributed indirectly to the CPI's growth in Assam in the sense that disenchantment with the Congress leadership brought a large number of youth under the influence of the communist ideology.[53] Even though the strike was not organized by the CPI itself, the strike appears to have received the full backing and support of the party and of its student wing.

CPI and the Peasant Movement in Assam

The system of land tenure in British Assam was not uniform. Along with the system of communal or clan ownership in the hills districts, private property rights in land also existed. Under the Settlement Rules of 1870, the Government, for the first time, categorically and unequivocally recognized the permanent, transferable and heritable rights in rupit (wet paddy) and bari (homestead) lands in private occupation.[54] Now, a complex problem facing the people of Assam was the pressure on land created by unchecked immigration from over-populated East Bengal, resulting in a clash of interests between the local people and the immigrants. To contain the conflict, a line was drawn to settle immigrants in segregated areas. But the Line System failed to settle the problem.[55] Local peasants refused to accept an open society lest their separate cultural heritage was eroded through the loss of their lands to the more enterprising immigrants.[56] A resolution adopted on this issue by the Assam unit of the CPI stated thus :

> "The very question of self-existence of the Assamese people as a distinct and growing

nationality now hinges on this problem, and naturally enough, the people of Assam are seriously perturbed with an intense desire for checking further immigration which has been the primary cause for complicating the question of land settlement".[57]

The CPI could not support in unequivocal terms the demand for a policy of wastelands settlement with the landless, irrespective of their race, creed and language. It had to concede that the Assamese people should have the first right to such lands in their own national homeland and that the problem required a political solution. However, it condemned the Government violence in dealing with the immigrant encroachers and their forcible eviction. But such pragmatic gestures were hardly meaningful. The CPI tried its best to remain above petty and communal considerations and suggested the following principles for acceptance by both Congress and Muslim League:

(i) Stop immigration;

(ii) Postpone evictions pending working out of planned settlement;

(iii) Withdraw voluntarily from 'Reserves' illegally encroached upon; and

(iv) Recognise the right of self-determination for the people of Assam and full democratic and cultural rights to the minorities.[58]

The bulk of the peasants in Assam, who had no surplus to sell, suffered from the war-time increase in the cost of living.[59] Bireshchandra Misra, a Congress stalwart turned Communist, explained the Communist ideology and the significance of the red flag under the cover of peasant meetings and drew the attention of the farmers as to how their counterparts in Soviet Russia established their own Government through united struggle.[60] The communists pointed out that despite India's participation in World War I, the plight of the poor and landless did not improve. It was thus proposed to them that they should not support the war nor contribute towards it either in cash or in kind.[61]

In the Brahmaputra Valley, particularly in Kamrup and Golaghat, the Communists mobilized their full strength to make their influence felt in the peasant front. The Communist groups also dominated most of the peasant conferences held after the declaration of war.[62] By the end of 1941, the Communist groups in the Kamrup district succeeded in bringing the peasants to the agitational path.[63] However, the overall growth of Kisan Sabhas in Assam remained sluggish through the war years.[64] The first conference of the CPI-controlled Assam Provincial Kisan Sabha was held at Thekeragaon in Nowgong district in 1946. It talked of peasant unity and wanted Gandhi and Jinnah to come to terms. But as Guha points out, it could suggest no agreeable political solution other than mere patchworks.[65]

In the Surma Valley, the prospect of an effective class organization on the basis of Hindu-Muslim unity was somewhat brighter, despite minor communal clashes engineered here and there. By 1945, a militant struggle for occupancy rights and for the abolition of certain feudal obligations developed among Nankars, peasants settled on rent-free lands in lieu of obligatory personal service to their Zamindars.[66] In Sylhet, the CPI was thus able to build up a united platform of Hindu and Muslim peasants in certain pockets of their influence against all provocations.[67]

The civil disobedience movement of the thirties eventually took the shape of an unprecedented mass uprising. In 1935, a "Ryot Sabha" was formed at the initiative of Krishna Nath Sarma and others. Later on, a section of disgruntled Congress workers formed a peasants' organization called the "Halowa Sangha". Subsequently, they formed alliances with the leftwingers of the Congress, including the Communists. Its name was changed in 1938 to the Golaghat Krishak Sabha at the initiative of Jadunath Saikia. This may be regarded as the beginning of the organized peasants' movement in Assam under a left leadership.[68] Under the auspices of the Golaghat Krishak Sabha, the third session of the Golaghat District Krishak Sanmilan was held at Kamargaon on 14th October, 1939. The Conference called upon the peasants to assemble under the Congress banner and demanded a 50 percent reduction in land revenue dues.[69]

Peasant agitation was organized in some places of the Brahmaputra Valley by the underground Communist League - a splinter group of the CPI which was later renamed after the parent body and remained so until it was finally designated as the Revolutionary Communist Party of India in 1943. The Assam Peasant and Labour Party (Krishak Banuva Panchayat) was formed as its open platform at a meeting of delegates from several districts, held at Gauhati on 2 May, 1940.[70]

In November, 1938, Saumyendranath Tagore, the founder of the Communist League, had visited Gauhati and met a group of student youth, associated with the Gauhati Vyayam Sangha. Already disillusioned with the Congress leadership, they were much impressed by Tagore's independent left platform, international experience and Marxism he talked of in the context of the Digboi strike and the general unrest.[71] Led by Haren Kalita, the Gauhati Vyayam Sangha Group joined the Communist League. An underground organizing committee of the League and an open Marxist Youth Study Club, styled 'Radical Institute', meanwhile, had come into existence at Gauhati.[72] The Progressive Union and the Radical Institute, between them, played a significant role in drawing the cream of Assamese students towards Marxism and the broad front of 'left' nationalism.[73] These propaganda activities culminated in the spread of leftist parties in general and the CPI in particular.

In February, 1943, the first conference of the Assam Communists was held secretly in the residence of Khageswar Tamuli at Golaghat. At that time, there were thirty-five party members in the Brahmaputra Valley. The Conference was attended by all members other than Dr. Binoy Chakravarty, Nilmoni Barthakur, Dhiren Dutta, Jagannath Bhattacharya and those who were then in prison. The conference elected the Assam Valley District Committee of CPI under the Bengal Provincial Committee with Jadu Saikia as the Secretary. A decision was also taken to shift the headquarters to Gauhati.[74]

The new committee faced two important organizational problems. First, it was felt that a district unit was necessary for more effective functioning. Accordingly, Jadu Saikia and Dadhi Mahanta wrote to the Bengal Committee, urging the need for a full-fledged Provincial Committee. Bhawani Sen, Muzaffar Ahmed and Biswanath Mukherjee, on behalf of the Bengal Committee appreciated the proposal of the Assam comrades, but went on to remind them that only the party Congress was authorized to give the final verdict on the issue of formation of a separate Provincial Committee. Hence, the Assam leaders were advised to wait for the first congress of the party scheduled to be held at Bombay in mid-1943. The second problem was regarding the wrong implementation of the People's War theory by some members of the party who addressed a gathering organized by the National

War Front set up by the British Government. The People's War Theory did not make it obligatory for the Communists to cooperate with the National War Front. The party, therefore, pulled up those who misinterpreted the CPI's policy and instructed them to work amongst trade union organizations.[75]

However, despite these problems, the CPI workers carried on with their activities. The Red Flag Railway Workers' Union became quite active in the Pandu-Gauhati, Lumding and Dibrugarh-Tinsukia areas.[76] During this period, an organization called Mahila Atma Raksha Samity (Women's Self Defence Committee) was set up at the initiative of women communists and sympathizers to face the Japanese aggression. Such committees sprang up in Dibrugarh, Shillong and Sylhet.[77]

In 1943, Salt became extremely scarce in Assam.[78] The Communists took the initiative and a joint movement was built up along with the Congress, Muslim League and other parties to fight against the scarcity of salt artificially created by the traders in collaboration with the Government's supply officials, including the British Deputy Commissioner in Dibrugarh. The movement later spread to other areas as well.[79]

In May, 1943, the first open congress of CPI was held in Bombay. This Congress paved the way for the formation of an All-India structure of party organizations. As desired by the Assam leaders, the Assam provincial organizing committee of the CPI was formed.[80] Biresh Misra was elected Secretary and Biswanath Mukherjee took charge of the Assam unit on behalf of the Central Committee. By the beginning of 1944, Achintya Bhattacharya, Secretary, Cachar District Congress Committee, joined the CPI and played a leading role in building up the party in Cachar and expanding its base in Kisan areas. Irawat Singh, the Manipur leader, who played a legendary role in the famous 'Rice Satyagraha' was influenced by the Marxist-Leninist ideology during his imprisonment. He was able to induct a large number of Manipuri youth into the party. He worked for sometime in Cachar among the local Manipur peasantry[81] as a result of which the entire Manipuri peasant belt of Cachar came under the party's influence. This enhanced the formation of a district unit of the party.[82]

The first district conference of the CPI was held in 1938 in Sylhet. Chitta Das was elected Secretary of the district committee. The party's weekly journal *Naya Duniya* was edited by Jyotirmoy Nandy[83] who was elected Congress Secretary in the second conference of the party. Biresh Misra, a leader of the district Congress and of the Congress Socialist Party (C.S.P.), came in close contact with the party as a result of his participation in mass movements along with communists. Subsequently, he joined the party in 1941 and then became the first Secretary of Assam Provincial Organizing Committee of CPI.[84] In 1941, a conference of the communist workers was held at Dacca-Dakshin, Sylhet, in which Surma Valley

District Committee of CPI under Bengal Provincial Committee was formed. On behalf of the Brahmaputra Valley comrades, Bishnu Bora attended the conference as fraternal delegate.[85] Thus, the CPI was able to draw in its ranks prominent Congress Socialist Party leaders who worked actively towards the party's development in Assam. The party also extended its sphere of influence beyond the Brahmaputra Valley by forming the Surma Valley District Committee of the CPI. The Congress Socialists and Communists in Assam came together to fight against the grouping scheme.[86] The Assam Provincial Organizing Committee of the CPI called the AICC Resolution a death-blow to Assam's birth right to decide her own constitution and her relations with Bengal and other provinces. It called upon the Assamese people and "their mighty Congress Organization" to break away from the compromising policy of the leadership.[87]

In course of its memorandum to the Cabinet Mission, the CPI emphasized its stand for an undivided federal India. But at the same time, it suggested that the proposed interim Government be entrusted with the task of setting up a boundary commission to re-draw the boundaries on the basis of natural ancient home-lands of every people.[88] The CPI's stand was perfectly in tune with J.V. Stalin's ideological formulation in 1912 that India was still a melting pot of several growing nationalities.[89]

Hill leaders like late J.J.M. Nichols Roy and others rendered support to their counterparts in the plains in opposing the Cabinet Mission proposal. T. Aliba Imti Ao, the Naga National Council leader, came out openly against the grouping scheme and offered to send a group of volunteers to prevent coercive occupation of land by immigrants during the so-called civil disobedience movement led by the Muslim League. Eventually, the Congress leadership was forced to reject the Cabinet Mission proposal. MacDonald Konger appealed to all the members of the Legislature belonging to Assam proper to cooperate with each other in imposing immediate measures for "stopping further immigration into the Assam Valley from outside and for evicting all encroachers from the reserves, thereby saving the peace-loving children of the soil from economic, social and political ruination".[90] Eventually the Congress leadership was forced to reject the Cabinet Mission proposal.[91] The role played by the communists in this struggle contributed towards mobilizing public opinion against the grouping scheme. The communists also made use of this opportunity to endear themselves to the Assamese people on a highly sensitive and sentimental issue.

Cultural activities organized in the form of songs, dances and drama in the languages of the indigenous people can play a very significant role in awakening the political consciousness and patriotic feelings of the people of a nation under foreign domination. The Indian People's Theatre Association was organized in May 1943, during the CPI's first congress in Bombay to inject communist ideology into Indian cultural life,[92] the inspiration being the glorious role played by the Chinese People's Theatre Movement in awakening consciousness among the Chinese people during the Anti-Japanese freedom struggle. Its role in the cultural regeneration of India cannot be underestimated. Many veteran artists and musicians rendered their services to the IPTA. Through the IPTA movement, the CPI was able to make breakthrough amongst the intellectuals in Assam. A number of poets, writers and musicians assembled under the party's banner.[93] The CPI claimed that one troupe that toured the country in 1943-44 collected Rs. 200,000 for the famine stricken people of Bengal.[94] The IPTA brought back the memories of forgotten heroes like U Tirot Sing, Kiang Nongbah, Piali Phukan, Maniram Dewan and other freedom fighters through its shadow plays.[95]

As the CPI began to establish itself firmly all over Assam, it was felt that the party should have an organ of its own. Accordingly, in 1946, the first CPI journal in Assamese, a weekly called *Natun Asam* was published from Gauhati with Dadhi Mahanta as its editor. This journal propagated the cause of the working class and repudiated the anti-communist slogans of the reactionaries. During the late forties, several books and pamphlets on Marxism including *Communist Manifesto* were published in Assamese by the CPI and also by Pragati Prakash Bhawan of RCPI. The propaganda activities conducted by *Natun Asam* and books and pamphlets on Marxism were instrumental for the popularization of scientific socialism and for education of the cadres.[96]

After 1947, the CPI spelt out the need to carry forward the revolution to a new stage - the stage of the completion of the unfinished anti-imperialist, anti-feudal tasks of rejuvenating and building a prosperous national economy, of ensuring better living standards for our people and enlarging and enriching the field of democracy, so as to open the road to socialism for them.[97] However, after 1947, a group of Trotskyites within the Communist Party discarded the very notion of India's independence as false and urged the importance of freedom through armed struggle and creation of liberated zones. B.T. Ranadive advocated a militant policy of violent insurrection and guerilla activity. Ranadive felt confident that the time was ripe and his was the responsibility to engineer the final revolution in India like the October uprising of 1917 in Russia.[98] The violent policy engineered by Ranadive thoroughly isolated the party from the masses. Taking advantage of the popular sentiment and the divisions within the party, the Congress leadership let loose a reign of terror. Hundreds of Communists in Assam were hauled up.[99]

The first provincial conference of the CPI was held at Gauhati in February, 1948, and attended by delegates from all districts of Assam. The conference did make some sound economic pronouncements and put forward viable solutions of national problems. An eighteen-member strong provincial committee was elected with Biresh Misra as its secretary.[100]

The deviationist tendencies among a section of the CPI caused concern to the International Communist Movement. The Cominform issued through its organ "For a lasting Peace, For a People's Democracy", of 27th January, 1950, a new directive to the Indian Communist Party. The new dictat called upon the working class to unite with all classes, parties, groups and organizations willing to fight the imperialists and their hirelings and to form a broad, nationwide front headed by the working class and its vanguard, the Communist Party.[101] It pointed out that while fighting reformism, the Party Centre committed certain errors in dogmatist and sectarian directions, which restricted the scope of the struggle of the workers and the toiling masses and prevented the mobilization of the broadest masses in the same.[102] This led to a decline of the Ranadive line.[103] In Assam, the fight against the Ranadive line was carried on by Jyotirmoy Nandy, Phani Bora, Dadhi Mahanta, Biren Dutta, Bijon Roy, Prafulla Misra and others.[104] At the end of 1952, the Union of India had its first general elections. Now, the Communist Party had managed in the first half of 1951 to patch up the differences in its ranks and put up a show of unity on the basis of the United Front Programme outlined by the Cominform Journal.[105]

In 1951, the reinstatement of the dissolved Assam Provincial Committee took place. Biresh Misra, who pursued the left adventurist line in Assam was removed and replaced by Phani Bora as the Secretary of the Committee.[106] In a meeting of party workers held at Gauhati, the draft programme of the party was discussed and efforts were made to reorganize the party.[107] During 1948-51, the party seemed to gain substantially in organizational sphere because many of the members worked as whole timers to build the party organization with renewed vigour. And as a result, in the General Election of 1952, the CPI candidate Gaurisankar Bhattacharya emerged winner from Gauhati Assembly constituency. As Dadhi Mahanta pointed out, the railway workers and the fighting Beltala peasantry voted for the party candidate. The urban Bengali middle class stood firmly behind the CPI because in the wake of the anti-Bengali disturbances at Gauhati in 1948, the party strongly defended the interests of the minorities. This victory enhanced the prestige of the party in Assam to a great extent.[108]

Meanwhile, in a provincial conference of R.C.P.I. held at Gauhati, a decision was taken to dissolve the party and merge with the CPI. The unification of the Communist movement resulted in the expansion of its mass base. The party won 4 seats in the 1957 General Election and Phani Bora came out as the winner in the 1959 Nowgong bye-election.[109]

The CPI participated actively in the oil refinery movement, food movement etc.[110] In 1960, came the demand for making Assamese the state language. As a result, Assamese-Bengali fractricidal riot broke out. While the CPI had no clear policy on the language question, it always fought against chauvinism. The CPI State Council met at Gauhati and under the guidance of the Central Committee, adopted a resolution according to which Assamese should be declared the State language of Assam, Bengali shall be the official language in Cachar upto district level and the hill districts shall have a language chosen by the hills people themselves. Most of these recommendations were eventually enshrined in the Assamese Language Act. The CPI's ambiguous position on the language issue, however, resulted in a setback for the party in Assam.[111]

In the 1962 General Election, the CPI was virtually routed out. The party stood unrepresented in the Assembly. The Party's role during the language disturbances could not impress progressive sections of the society.[112] In October, 1962, the Chinese Army crossed the Mcmahon Line and advanced to the foothills of North-Eastern Frontier Province (NEFA). The CPI condemned the Chinese action, but the pro-Peking section within the CPI opposed the party line. In Assam, hundreds of Communists were detained under the Defence of India Rules (DIR) and the police was given a free hand.[113] All these factors contributed to the party's rout in the 1962 Election.

Split in Communist Movement and its effect on the CPI in Assam

Early in 1959 began the people's revolt in Tibet as a result of which the Dalai Lama and thousands of Tibetans had to seek refuge in India. The Communists were on the horns of a dilemma. On the one hand, they could not admit, as Communists, the possibility of a Socialist country indulging in aggression. On the other hand, anxious to retain the support and esteem of the people as a national party, they could not but take into consideration their anger and resentment against China. The differences that existed in the party now became more manifest and it was clearly divided into two groups, one of which sought inspiration from Moscow while the other sought it from Peking. Owing to these differences and also for ideological reasons, the Communist Party could not adopt anything but an equivocal position.[114] When China crossed the Mcmahon Line in October 1962, again a very difficult situation was created for the Communists. It took the party full two weeks to adopt a resolution on the situation. The resolution characterized the Chinese action as aggression and called upon the people to unite for the defence of the country. This resolution sharpened the division of the party into two groups - one left and the other right.[115]

The Assam State Council of the CPI met in June 1964 at Krishnai, Goalpara, to take disciplinary action against Achintya Bhattacharya, Biresh Misra,

Nandeswar Talukdar and Suren Hazarika, the four Council members, for their anti-party activities. These four members in collaboration with some others formed a separate party committee of C.P.I. (M) in Assam.[116]

But despite the split in the communist movement, the CPI gained in influence and organizational strength during this period. In the general election held in Assam in 1967, the CPI captured 8 seats (seven on party ticket and one as independent). Six independent members joined the CPI parliamentary group in the Assembly.[117] The party M.L.As' performance in the Assembly, their attitude of solidarity with the cause of the minorities, detection of corruption and nepotism of the Congress Government with documentary evidence, formation and expansion of mass organizations and support for mass movements enabled the party to assert considerable influence in Assam during that period.[118] In 1969, the Assam unit of the CPI celebrated its Silver Jubilee. At the time of the split, the total membership of the party was 3,000 only. But in 1969, the primary membership rose to more than 7,000 including in Meghalaya.[119]

Origin and Growth of the CPI in the Hills

Under-administered and kept in seclusion as the museum specimens of 'backward tracts', there was practically no political development in the hills of Assam, except for the Khasi-Jaintia Hills District, until the end of World War II.[120] All India political parties and organizations had been making some attempts since 1938 to draw the hills people into their folds but with little success. They had no access to the 'excluded areas' or even to the interior of the 'partially excluded areas'. As a result, their contacts were limited to Shillong and to the hills students studying in other district towns.[121]

Christianity and literacy made rapid progress in the twentieth century. Because of the deep religiosity of the hills people and the fierce opposition of the church towards communists, the latter's influence on the Christian hills students was neither stable nor deep. What appealed to them most was the communist approach to the national question. They collected from bookshops at Shillong, Gauhati and Jorhat dozens of copies of such Marxist publications as were relevant to the subject, particularly copies of the USSR Constitution, for the consumption of their reading public at home.[122] In order to cultivate Marxist ideas among the Khasis, the Shillong unit of the CPI published a number of pamphlets in the Khasi language such as "Ka Jinglaitluid ha ka Niam ha ka U.S.S.R.". (Religion in the Soviet Union) and "Ia ka Jaid Bynriew ha Russia" (How National Question was solved in U.S.S.R.). The Soviet concept of a multinational State (each nationality therein with a formal right to secede) and of autonomous regions was to their liking, afraid as they were of domination by the plains people. The impact of the

USSR Constitution was soon to be seen on the growth of their group consciousness.[123]

In 1937, Soumen Tagore, the founder of the Communist League, came to Shillong and stayed for two months during which he helped a left-oriented Congressman, Kiriti Chaudhuri, to organize the Municipal workers of Shillong. The efforts in this direction culminated in the formation of Shillong Municipal Workers' Union with Swami Saradananda as President and Kiriti Chaudhuri as Secretary.[124] The Government Press Workers, too, were organized under a Union. The Municipal Workers struck work in 1938. This may be regarded as the first workers' strike in Shillong. In 1940, the Government Press Workers also resorted to strike.[125] Students' Federation expressed solidarity with the striking workers.[126]

During the late thirties, several all-India leaders with leftist inclinations visited Shillong. This led to the radicalization of students in Shillong. Subhas Chandra Bose,[127] founder of the Forward Bloc, came to Shillong in 1937 and addressed public gatherings. He also visited Shillong in 1938. Soli Batlivwala and Sajjad Zaheer of CPI addressed public meetings in Shillong in 1939. Shillong Students' Federation was formed in 1938 with Sailen Neogy as Secretary.[128] In 1940, the first joint conference of Assam Valley, Surma Valley and Shillong Students' Federations was held at Opera Hall, Shillong, under the presidentship of Humayun Kabir. The conference was addressed by Biswanath Mukherjee (CPI) and Biswanath Dube (Bolshevik Party), Ajoy Bhattacharya and Gaurishankar Bhattacharya.[129]

In 1939-40, Barin Dutta, a member of the Communist Party group that functioned in Sylhet since 1938, visited Shillong while he was underground and through party classes, initiated a group of students and youth of Shillong to Marxism-Leninism. Towards the end of 1942, this group was transformed into a party cell and by the middle of 1943, the Shillong Local Committee of CPI was formed with Benubinode Chaudhuri as Secretary. Shyamapada Dutta, Bijon Roy, Anjali Das, Benubinode Chaudhury, Himangshu Gupta and others played an important role in the party's formation.[130] The Shillong unit established links with the students of different hills of Assam and propagated progressive ideas, but failed to build any party organization in the hills. Through its bookstall "Friends of the Soviet Union" (later Booklands), the party circulated thousands of copies of Marxist books in Khasi and Jaintia Hills, Naga Hills and Mizo Hills.[131]

It may be noted that the Shillong local unit of the CPI formed at the initiative of local Bengalis could not recruit tribal cadres excepting one or two during the war years. However, the Students' Federation was able to establish rapport with the hills students in various colleges of Assam and Calcutta. For example, G.G. Swell, a Khasi student then studying in Calcutta, was a member of the Working Committee of the Bengal Provincial Students' Association in 1945.[132] At the same time, the Assam Hill Students' Federation was formed in Assam, with T. Aliba Imti Ao, a Naga student, as its Secretary. This body, jointly with Assam affiliate of the AISF, organized the All-Assam Students' Educational Conference in 1946 at Shillong, which adopted a charter of demands for the spread of education in the province in general and the hills in particular. Several tribal students, who actively participated in this conference, later emerged as local leaders in their respective regions.[133] The student wing of the CPI thus played an important role in politicizing the students of the hills of Assam. The Shillong unit of the CPI proposed autonomy for the Hills and this policy was eventually adopted by the all-India leadership of the party for all the tribal areas of India.[134] This point will be elaborated in the second chapter.

During 1944-45, the Shillong unit of the CPI organized the workers of Commercial Carrying Company, the Grade IV Government Employees' Association, Motor Workers' Union, Shop Assistants' Association etc. The party revitalized the Ministerial Employees' Association as a militant organization. The party was actively involved in the Municipal Strike and the Post and Telegraph Employees' Strike of 1946. It also organized the women into the Mahila Atma Raksha Samity (Women's Self-Defence Committee). Benubinode Chaudhury, Paresh Das,

Binoy Lahiri, Hiru Datta, Debabrata Das and Benoy Deb played an active role in the formation of trade unions.[135] It is interesting to note that all the party activists were Bengali in a town dominated by Khasis.

The Shillong unit of the CPI spearheaded the food movement in the capital against scarcity of rice and soaring prices in 1966. In the police firing that followed, a student was killed and many injured while a large number of Communist workers and sympathizers were detained under the Defence of India Rules. The party also organized the First Oil Refinery movement in Shillong. During the Bangladesh Liberation Struggle, the party units in Khasi and Garo Hills played a key role in assisting the liberation movement. The Bangladesh Mukti Sangram Sahayak Samity was organized on the initiative of the Shillong Committee of the CPI to help the Freedom Fighters in all possible ways. The Samity gave the call for a Shillong Bandh on April 7, 1971.[136]

In 1950, the Hajong tribals of Mymensingh district (erstwhile East Pakistan) inspired by Moni Singh rose in rebellion against feudal oppression. The Hajong Communists formed a parallel administration by liberating a number of villages. On being resisted by the Pakistani army from advancing farther, they took refuge in Baghmara[137] in the Garo Hills border and continued their struggle against Pakistani authorities under the command of Lalit Sarkar and late Padmalochan Sarkar.

Subsequently, they became permanent settlers of the Indian Union.[138] On the initiative of Lalit Sarkar, a unit of the Communist Party was set up in the Garo Hills in the early sixties. Robin Rema, a preacher turned Communist, is a prominent leader of the party's Garo Hills Unit.[139] The Garo Hills party unit fought for three assembly seats in 1967 and for two in 1972, but failed to win any seats. The party organized the first ever Kisan demonstration in 1969, a landmark in the Kisan movement in Garo Hills. It has also organized some trade unions in Garo Hills.[140] Late Padmalochan Sarkar, one of the leaders of the Hajong rebellion, settled down in Khasi Hills. He, along with Chandramohan Hajong and Raimohan Hajong[141], made a valuable contribution to the formation of the Communist Party in South Khasi Hills.[142]

CPI in Assam and Naga Struggle

The CPI, while advocating cultural and regional autonomy for the Naga people, had strongly opposed any military solution of the Naga problem and had emphasized the need for a negotiated settlement between the Government of India and the Naga National Council.[143] The CPI had broadly backed the demands submitted by the N.N.C. in the form of an ultimatum in November, 1947.[144] In the Memorandum of November 1947, addressed to the Prime Minister of India,[145] the Assam Provincial Organizing Committee of the CPI maintained that the demand for a sovereign independent Nagaland put forward by the N.N.C. was, in effect, a demand for greater autonomy and not for secession from the Indian Union. Since the tone of the CPI Memorandum exhibited a great degree of sympathy for the N.N.C. led movement, the CPI was subsequently criticized for encouraging the secessionist movement in the Naga Hills.[146] According to Udayan Misra, the ideological standpoint on the problem of nationalities in India certainly played a role in the party's assessment of the Naga struggle in the fifties.[147]

By the mid-fifties, however, the CPI insisted that the Nagas could realize their destiny as a separate nationality only within the Indian Union.[148] Thus, the ambiguity which marked the CPI's 1947 memorandum had, by the mid-fifties, been replaced by a call for regional autonomy for the Nagas within the Indian Union to be worked out through negotiations with "all patriotic Naga leaders".[149]

Formation of the Meghalaya State Committee of the CPI

When the Autonomous State of Meghalaya was born on April 2, 1970, it was felt that the formation of a full-fledged State was only a matter of time. The new State eventually came into being on January 21, 1972, at a time when the political scenario in the region was relatively peaceful. As the inauguration of the Autonomous State of Meghalaya took place in 1970, the Meghalaya Co-ordination Committee of the CPI was formed to carry on the activities of the party in the new administrative and political order.[150] In the next chapter, we propose to examine the issue of the Hill State in order to examine the CPI's stand on regional aspirations for autonomy and statehood, because fortunes of all political parties in Meghalaya seem to be connected closely with their stand on this issue.

References

1. For a discussion on this period, see Satyabrata Ray Chaudhuri, *Leftist Movements in India: 1917-1947,* (Calcutta, 1977), p. 45.
2. Here, we are talking about the Muhajirin, fanatical Muslims who left India in protest against the Afghan War of 1919 and reached Tashkent in September 1920. They accepted Marxism as their creed after joining the Communist University at Moscow.
3. See Muzaffar Ahmad, *The Communist Party of India and Its Formation Abroad,* (Calcutta, 1962), pp. 27-28.
4. *Ibid.,* p. 33.
5. *Ibid.,* pp. 87-88.
6. *The Communist International Documents 1919-43,* (London, 1956), Vol. II, BIIA, Editor's Note, p. 11.
7. Satyabrata Ray Chaudhuri, *op.cit.,* p. 65.
8. *Ibid.,* pp. 71-72.
9. Muzaffar Ahmad, *The Communist Party of India—Years of Formation* (Calcutta, 1959), pp. 28-36.

10. See, G. Adhikari (ed.), *Documents of the History of the Communist Party of India,* Vol. I, 1917-1922, (New Delhi, 1971), p. 3.
11. *Loc.cit.*
12. Prafulla Misra, "The Communist Party of India in Assam: A Brief History" *in North East Quarterly,* Vol. 2, No. l, July 1984, pp. 5-6.
13. *Ibid.,* p. 6.
14. M. R. Masani, *The Communist Party of India—A Short History,* (Bombay, 1967), p. 24.
15. *Ibid.,* p. 26, and Satyabrata Rai Choudhury, *op.cit.,* p. 84.
16. Jadu Saikia, "Mor Communist Howar Smriti" in Bharatar Communist Party, Assam Rajya Parishad, *Rupali Jayanti Sonwaran,* 1969, pp. 2-3.
17. Bishnu Borah, "Asamat Communist Party Gathanar Smriti" in Bharatar Communist Party, Assam Rajya Parishad, *Rupali Jayanti Sonwaran,* 1969, p. 8.
18. For a discussion on this, see S. Borah, "The Cunningham Circular as a Catalyst in the Civil Disobedience Movement (1930)" in *Proceedings of the N.E. India History Association,* Second Session, (Dibrugarh, 1981).
19. Prafulla Misra, "Communist Movement in Assam", *North Eastern Affairs,* Shillong, July-September, 1972, p. 24.
20. *Loc.cit.*
21. *Loc.cit.*
22. For details see, *Ibid.*

23. *Loc.cit.*
24. For a discussion on Assam Chhatra Sanmilan, see Meeta Deka, *'Student Movements in Assam 1905-1947'*, published in *North East Quarterly,* Vol. 2, No. 2, January-March, 1987, and Vol. 2, No. 3, April-June, 1987.
25. P. Misra, *op.cit.,* p. 26
26. "No. 1179: Notes on the political activities of Praneshchandra Biswas" and his written testimony obtained by Amalendu Guha on 12 June, 1973, in Shillong; Misra, *"Communist Movement in Assam', op.cit.,* p. 29; File No. Λ 8 (8A)-40: "Notes on the political activities of Bistoo Bora", Police Deptt. Special Branch, Government of Assam, Shillong.
27. 6 December, *Assam Legislative Assembly Proceedings (1941),* pp. 1401-24; *Assam Tribune,* 12 December, 1941; *The Golden Jubilee Volume,* Cotton College, (Gauhati, 1951-52), p. 73.
28. Tarun Sen Deka, *'Asomar Biplabi Kommunist Sambandhe Esar' Rupali Jayanti Sonwaran,* 1969, p. 3
29. For a discussion on this point, see *People's War,* 6 September, 1942.
30. *Ibid.*
31. Amalendu Guha, *op. cit.,* p. 277.
32. *Loc. cit., n.* 39.
33. *Loc. cit.*
34. P. Misra, *'Communist Movement in Assam', Op.cit.,* p. 32.
35. Amalendu Guha, *op.cit.,* p. 308.

36. Satyabrata Ray Chaudhuri, *op.cit.,* p. 186.

    For details on this point, see B. Shiva Rao, *The Industrial Workers in India,* (London, 1939), p. 19.

37. Amalendu Guha, *Op.cit.,* p. 237.
38. Satyabrata Ray Chaudhuri, *Op.cit.,* p. 192.
39. *Loc.cit.*
40. Overstreet and Windmiller, *Communism in India,* (Bombay, 1960), p. 369. For an account of this, see also Philip Spratt, *Blowing up India,* (Calcutta, 1955), p. 32.
41. For details, see R. K. Das, *Labour Movement in India,* (Berlin, 1923), pp. 30-40.
42. For an account of the Strikes of Assam during this period, see *Royal Commission on Labour of India, Written Evidence,* Vol. VI, Part 1, *Assam Labour Enquiry Committee Report 1921-22* (Government of Assam, Arbuthnott Committee), pp. 6-8; Sanat Kr. Bose, *'Strikes in Assam Tea Gardens in 1921'* *New Age,* August, 1953. Also see Amalendu Guha, *op.cit.,* pp. 131-132.
43. Amalendu Guha, *Op.cit.,* p. 241.
44. Prafulla Misra, *'The Communist Party of India in Assam'*, *Op.cit.,* p. 15
45. *Assam Administrative Report,* 1938-39, p. 1.
46. *Assam Tribune,* 3 December, 1943 and *Ibid.,* 1 June, 1945. Also *People's War,* 9 January, 1944.
47. *People's Age,* 12 May 1946 and also its election supplement, 17 February, 1946.
48. Amalendu Guha, *Op.cit.,* p. 237.

49. M. N. Mukherji, *Report of the Committee of Enquiry into the Affairs at Digboi* (25 November, 1939); *Assam Administrative Report,* 1938-39, p. ii; *IAR* (Indian Annual Register), January-June 1939, Vol. I, pp. 256 and 357-58.
50. P. Misra, *"Communist Movement in Assam', op.cit.,* p. 26.
51. Bishnu Bora, *op. cit.,* p. 8.
52. P. Misra, *'The Communist Party of India in Assam', op.cit.,* p. 16.
53. *Loc.cit.*
54. A. Guha, *Op.cit.,* pp. 47-48.
55. *Ibid.,* p. 206.
56. *Ibid.,* p. 298.
57. *"Resolution on land settlement and eviction in Assam", Assam Fights for Freedom and Democracy: Draft Resolutions of Assam Communists* (Assam Provincial Organizing Committee, C.P.I., Gauhati, n.d.), pp. 41-50.
58. *Loc.cit.*
59. A. Guha, *Op.cit.,* p. 298.
60. *Assam Police Abstracts of Intelligence* (APAI), No. 279, Sylhet, 17 February, 1940.
61. *Ibid.*
62. H. K. Barpujari, *Political History of Assam 1940-1947* (Vol. Three), (Gauhati, 1980), p. 145.
63. *APAI,* No. 1883, Kamrup, 1 November, 1941.
64. *People's War,* 19 July, 1942.
65. Amalendu Guha, *Op.cit.,* p. 300.

66. *Loc.cit.*

67. *Ibid.,* pp. 300-301. The account is based on Amalendu Guha's interview with Jyotirmoy Nandy in Calcutta on 3 August 1974; Ajay Bhattacharya, *Nankar Vidroha,* Vol. I, (A book in Bengali, Dacca 1973).

68. For details, see, Jadu Saikia, *Op.cit.,* pp. 3-4.

69. CPI, Assam State Council, *Silver Jubilee Souvenir* (In Assamese, May 1969, Gauhati), p. 3; *Assam Tribune,* 27 October, 1939.

70. For a discussion on this point, see A. Guha, *op.cit.,* p. 249.

71. *Ibid.,* p. 253.

72. *Ibid.,* pp. 253-254. Amalendu Guha's interview with Haridas Deka, 27 February, 1974, Gauhati.

73. A. Guha, *Op.cit.,* p. 254.

74. Dadhi Mahanta, *Jatiya Mukti Sangramar Patabhumit Bharatar Communist Party,* (Gauhati, 1969), published on the occasion of Silver Jubilee Celebration of the CPI in Assam, p. 48.

75. *Ibid.,* pp. 48-49.

76. For details, see Barpujari, *op. cit.,* pp. 149 and 191-193.

77. Prafulla Misra, *'Communist Movement in Assam',* *op.cit.,* p. 30.

78. For a discussion on scarcity of salt and other essential commodities in Assam and the CPI's stand, see Barpujari, *op.cit.,* pp. 165-167, 167-170 and 188-189.

79. Prafulla Misra, 'Communist Movement in Assam', *op.cit.,* p. 30, Misra's interview with Bishnu Bora in 1972 at Shillong.
80. See Jyotirmoy Nandy, *'Mor Koifiyat'*, *Rupali Jayanti Sonwaran,* 1969, p. 18.
81. Amalendu Guha, *op.cit.,* p. 295.
82. P. Misra, *'The Communist Party of India in Assam"*, *op.cit.,* p. 21.
83. Jyotirmoy Nandy, "Asamat Party Pratisthar Joranir Dinborar Smriticharan", *Janamat,* December 22, 1975, p. 12.
84. *Ibid.,* pp. 12-13.
85. Prafulla Misra, 'The Communist Party of India in Assam', *op.cit.,* p. 22.
86. For detail, see Guha, *op.cit.,* pp. 309-315.
87. *Assam Fight for Freedom and Democracy: Draft Resolutions of Assam Communists* (Assam Provincial Organizing Committee, CPI, Gauhati, n.d.)
88. *CPI Memorandum of 15 April quoted in IAR* (January-June 1946), Vol. I, pp. 220-21.
89. J. V. Stalin, as cited by R. Palme Dutt, *India Today* (2nd Indian edn, Calcutta, 1970), p. 473.
90. *APAI,* 1944-45, No. 708, *Khasi and Jaintia Hills,* 31 March, 1945.
91. For further details, see D. C. Gupta, *Indian National Movement,* (New Delhi, 1970), pp. 255-257 and 260.
92. Overstreet and Windmiller, *op.cit.,* pp. 435-436.
93. For details, see P. Misra, 'The Communist Party of India in Assam', *op.cit.,* p. 23.

94. *People's Age,* IV (January 6, 1946), p. 12.
95. P. Misra, 'The Communist Party of India in Assam', *op.cit.,* p. 23.
96. See Misra, "Communist Movement in Assam", *op. cit.,* p. 32.
97. For details, see M.R. Masani, *op.cit.,* pp. 70 and 73.
98. *Loc.cit.*
99. Phani Bora, "Asamat Communist Partyr Pachish Bachar" in CPI, Assam State Council, *Silver Jubilee Souvenir* (in Assamese, May 1969, Gauhati), p. 25.
100. Dadhi Mahanta, *Jatiya Mukti Sangramar* etc., *op.cit.,* p. 53.
101. See *The Communist* (Quoted in a statement of the Editorial Board of this monthly journal of the CPI) February-March, 1950.
102. *Ibid.*
103. See, M. R. Masani, *op.cit.,* p. 85.
104. See Jyotirmoy Nandy, *"Mor Koifiyat", op.cit.,* pp. 19-20. Also see Phani Bora, *"Asamat Communist Partyr* etc.", *op.cit.,* p. 25.
105. M. R. Masani, *op.cit.,* p. 110.
106. Dadhi Mahanta, *Jatiya Mukti Sangramar Patabhumit* etc., *op.cit.,* p. 57.
107. *Loc.cit.*
108. *Loc.cit.*
109. It is interesting to note that he won the Nowgong seat by defeating the prominent Congress leader and former Minister for Education in Assam, Devkanta Baruah.

110. Dadhi Mahanta, *op.cit.,* p. 58.
111. *Ibid.,* pp. 58-59.
112. *Ibid.,* pp. 59-60.
113. P. Misra, 'Communist Movement in Assam', *op.cit.,* p. 38.
114. M. R. Masani, *Op.cit.,* Appendix by V. B. Karnik, p. 252.
115. *Ibid.,* p. 258. Also see Mohan Ram, *Indian Communism: Split Within A Split,* (New Delhi, 1969), Chapter V.
116. Dadhi Mahanta, *op.cit.,* p. 62.
117. *Ibid.,* p. 63.
118. *Loc.cit.*
119. Phani Bora, 'Asamat Communist Partyr Pachish Bachar', *op.cit.,* p. 25.
120. A. Guha, *op.cit,* p. 321.
121. *Ibid.,* p. 323.
122. See Prafulla Misra, 'Communist Movement in Assam', *op.cit.,* p. 37. Also see Amalendu Guha, *op.cit.,* p. 324. Information obtained by Guha from the relevant bookshops.
123. *Loc.cit.*
124. Interview with Prafulla Misra, dated 2nd March 1988. His discussions with Kiriti Chaudhuri, late Hiru Bhattacharya and late Sushil Bhadra who were connected with the said Union.
125. *Ibid.,* Misra's discussion with Sushil Bhadra who played an important role in organizing the strike.
126. Misra, 'Communist Movement in Assam', *op.cit.,* p. 36.

127. Subhas Chandra Bose, though not a Communist, certainly had radical views on socio-political issues. He founded 'Forward Bloc', a party with leftist leanings.

128. Misra, *op.cit,* p. 36.

129. Interview with Prafulla Misra, dated 2nd March, 1988. Misra, who was in Shillong at that time, met Humayun Kabir when he came to Shillong.

130. P. Misra, *'Communist Movement in Assam', op.cit.,* p. 37.

131. *Loc.cit.*

132. A. Guha, *op.cit.,* p. 323.

133. S. Chaube, *Hill Politics in North East India,* (Calcutta, 1973), pp. 73 and 141. Also P. Misra, 'Communist Movement in Assam', *op.cit.,* p. 37.

134. *'Programme of the Communist Party of India', op.cit.,* pp. 58-59. While discussing the party's policies regarding the tribal problem, the CPI programme stated that the national democratic government will give regional autonomy to the tribal areas inhabited by the tribal peoples.

135. P. Misra, 'Communist Movement in Assam', *op.cit.,* p. 37.

136. *Ibid.,* p. 38.

137. *Janamat,* 29 November, 1965, p. 4. For discussion on Hajong rebellion, see Pramatha Gupta, *Tribal People in Liberation Struggle* (Calcutta, 1983), pp. 69-98.

138. P. Misra, 'Communist Movement in Assam', *op.cit.,* pp. 37-38.

139. *Ibid.,* p. 38.

140. *Loc.cit.*
141. Interview with Prafulla Misra dated the 30th May, 1987.
142. Misra, *op.cit.*, p. 38.
143. Udayan Misra, *'The CPI and the Naga Struggle: Initial Years'*, in *North East Quarterly,* April-June, 1987, p. 34.
144. Ultimatum submitted by the Naga National Council to the Government of India, November 4, 1947.
145. Memorandum submitted to the Prime Minister of India by the Assam Provincial Committee of the CPI, November 24, 1947.
146. P. Misra, 'Communist Movement in Assam', *op.cit.,* p. 37.
147. Udayan Misra, *op.cit.,* p. 39. For a discussion on the CPI's Resolution regarding the nationality issue, see Mohan Ram, *Indian Communism,* (New Delhi, 1969), pp. 14-16 and 60-65.
148. See Phani Bora, *Nagas: The Real Story,* New Delhi, 1956.
149. "End this Miniature War in Naga Hills", *New Age,* July 1, 1956.
150. P. Misra, *'Communist Movement in Assam', op.cit.,* p. 38.

2

Demand of the Hill State and the Role of the CPI

The issues connected with the formation of a hill state had greatly exercised the minds of the people of the areas which later came to be known as the State of Meghalaya. The positions taken by various political parties on this issue greatly influenced their political prospects in Meghalaya. It would, therefore, be necessary to examine the CPI's position on this issue for an understanding of the party's political influence or lack of it in Meghalaya.

British administration in the tribal areas of North East India functioned primarily through the traditional chiefs, whose statutory recognition created vested interests. Separatist demands, wherever raised, have been sponsored by the powerful class of officers and the chiefs. According to S. K. Chaube, the outstanding aspects of the hills problem is political, the economic foundations of which can be traced not only in 'the Hills-peoples' long-standing grievances but also in the aspirations for a new destiny. In short, the Hills problem is a problem of growth which under special circumstances, has been articulated in political movements.[1]

Towards the end of the war, when the talk of transfer of power was in the air, some British civil servants and other interested quarters began to toy with the idea of a 'Crown Colony' consisting of all the contiguous hill areas of Burma and Assam.[2] To prepare the ground for such a possibility, some British officials in charge of the hills districts, took initiative in forming district level political bodies in which the tribal elite could participate. In the atmosphere of an anti-colonial upsurge all over India, it was but natural that the idea of a 'Crown Colony' or guided participation in politics did not appeal to the tribal mind.[3] However, the official efforts were successful to the extent of kindling an urge for autonomy and political participation and above all, nurturing the seeds of suspicion in tribal minds against their more developed neighbours in the plains.[4]

In the hills of Assam, as Amalendu Guha says, communal ownership over land was progressively giving way to the rise of private property during the twentieth century and even earlier.[5] The formation of an educated Christian elite helped the process. During the war years, when the panic-stricken immigrant shopkeepers and petty traders left the hills, circumstances compelled some local hillmen to take up these lucrative professions as well as petty war contracts. Thus, there emerged a small stratum of middle class people of local origin, which was not in existence there before, except in the Khasi-Jaintia Hills. Besides, the war time contacts with soldiers from many provinces and from many nations exposed the hillmen to the world outside and allowed them to be politicized. Lastly, Guha points out that the partition of the country largely disrupted the hills' economy, since some parts of the Garo, Mizo, Khasi and Jaintia Hills had long been economically more integrated with Eastern Bengal than with the plains of Assam. People in these areas had to undergo untold hardships because of this disruption of their normal trade channels. This experience, too, further strengthened their urge for local autonomy.[6]

In a meeting held in Shillong on 16 June, 1954, the members of the Executive Committees of the Autonomous District Councils of the Garo Hills, the Khasi and Jaintia Hills, the Lushai Hills (Mizo Hills) and the North Cachar Hills District Council, pleaded for the establishment of a separate Hill State on the ground that there was no adequate safeguard for the preservation of the identity of the hill people in the Sixth Schedule. The meeting decided to demand the constitution of a separate state for all the hill areas of Assam to be known as the Eastern Hill State.[7]

At the end of the Conference, a somewhat vague memorandum was drafted. The memorandum offered the comment that under the existing set-up, the Hills peoples disliked Congress, but they would welcome 'good All-India Organizations' including the Congress, after they would have achieved the Hill

State covering the six autonomous districts. At the same time, a set of suggestions for amendment of the Sixth Schedule was sent to the members of Parliament.[8] The hill leaders, however, did not explain why they did not like the Congress during the Hill State Movement and how overnight they would became admirers of the Congress after the creation of a State. This raised the question - was the demand for hill state a political move for a different goal? It appears that the hill state would have fulfilled the political aspirations of the tribal elite. Although the aspirations of different tribes were not exactly identical due to differences at the levels of educational and cultural development, the general need to dissociate themselves from Assam seemed to have been felt by almost the entire tribal leadership of composite Assam because the hill state seemed to offer better prospects for political autonomy entailing major benefits for this section of the tribal society.

The next step was an Assam Hills Tribal Leaders' Conference held at Tura, in Garo Hills, on October 6-8, 1954. On October 6, the Conference unanimously desired 'a separate State for the Autonomous Districts of Assam' and decided that a memorandum be submitted to the States Reorganization Commission. An appeal was sent to the leaders of all the tribal organizations and parties of the autonomous districts to sign the memorandum, adopted in the conference, pressing for a Hill State. The appeal met with a cold response in many districts.[9] The States Reorganization Commission, while rejecting the demand, observed:

> "Generally speaking, the United Mikir and North Cachar Hills and the Lushai Hills are not in favour of a separate hill state and the district council in the Lushai Hills and the Kerbia Durbar (Mikir National Council) are in favour of the status quo. The agitation in favour of a hill state is, therefore, confined virtually to the Garo and Khasi and Jaintia Hills".[10]

The rejection of the Hill State demand by the SRC was, however, not compensated by the enlargement of the powers of the District Councils. On August 28, 1955, when Prime Minister Nehru visited Shillong, a deputation of hill leaders met him to stress that the hills peoples were 'primarily concerned with social and economic development' in the Hills. The economic backwardness of the people created a fear-complex and suspicion in them, which could be removed by an Eastern Hills State. Imposition of Assamese would mean too many languages for the school children. The deputation advocated Hindi as the regional language of Assam to solve it. They wanted more opportunities in the Hills for technical education, social service and learning of Hindi, and demanded a separate Public Works Department for them.[11] While the demand for technical education seems awkward in the absence of opportunities for technical jobs, the rest of the demands voiced by the deputation sound somewhat paradoxical. The demand for a separate P.W.D. for the hills smacks of vested interest in construction works on the part of the emerging hill elite.[12]

On October 26-28, 1955, another conference of the hill leaders was held at Aizawl where the Eastern India Tribal Union was born. Before setting up the EITU, the conference expressed 'grave concern' at the SRC's inability 'to appreciate the aspiration and demand of the tribal people of this part of the country' and again called for the bringing of all hills under one administration.[13] On November 1, 1955, a memorandum was submitted to Home Minister, G.B. Pant, visiting Shillong.

The poor performance of the Congress in the 1957 election gave impetus to the Hills movement. Congress lost all the five seats in the United Khasi-Jaintia Hills, three seats in Garo Hills and one seat each in the Mikir Hills and North Cachar Hills. Meanwhile, Bishnuram Medhi was replaced as Chief Minister of Assam by Bimala Prasad Chaliha. Of all the Assam leaders, Chaliha had been singularly fortunate in commanding the confidence of the minorities in Assam, including the Hills peoples. At Chaliha's invitation, Captain Williamson Sangma became a Cabinet Minister in charge of the Tribal Areas Department.[14] The overwhelming success of hill parties like EITU, Garo National Council, United Mizo Freedom Organization, the Mizo Union etc. in the polls generated a popular mandate for the hill state.

Now, something happened in 1960 which accelerated the movement for a Hill State. The Assam Provincial Congress Committee (APCC) met on 22 April, 1960 and directed the Chief Minister (Chaliha) to declare Assamese as the State language. The immediate reaction to this decision was the meeting of All Assam Hill Leaders' Conference at Tura, Garo Hills, on 28 April, 1960, which vehemently opposed the decision of the APCC. It did not demand a separate state, but demanded the amendment of the Sixth Schedule.[15]

Meanwhile, Sangma's participation in the Chaliha Cabinet, backed by B.M. Pugh, created bad blood in the EITU. With the backing of Sangma, Pugh convened an annual conference of the EITU, on April 27-28, 1960. Significantly enough, the Hill State demand did not figure in the agenda of the Conference.[16]

However, the opposite camp in the EITU was moving towards an extremist stance. Hoover Hynniewta, the MP from the Assam Hills, had strongly raised the demand for a Hill State in April, 1958. The stage was now set for a split in the Hills movement even before it was really organized. In fact, the Hill State Movement was not born until the middle of 1960, when the Hills parties were in real disarray. It was the language issue which helped them to unite on a common platform, following the outbreak of violence between the Assamese speaking and Bengali speaking communities in the Assam plains.[17]

In June, 1960, Sangma called for a conference of all leaders of all the political parties in the hill areas. The conference unanimously resolved to oppose the Official Language Bill. It also resolved to form the All Party Hill Leaders' Conference (APHLC).[18]

In September, 1960, the APHLC Council of Action issued an ultimatum to the Assam Chief Minister. In October, Sangma resigned his cabinet post. On the night of October 24, 1960, the Assembly sat specially and adopted the Language Bill. On November 16-18, 1960, the third All Party Hill Leaders' Conference met at Haflong in North Cachar which demanded 'the immediate creation of a separate Hill State'. Chaube says that though the language issue provided the ground for the Hill State movement, its substance was the hillman's desire for an equal status with the Assamese plains people.[19] It may be argued in this context that creation of a hill state or transfer of political power from the Assamese elite to the Khasi, Jaintia or Garo elite could not be expected to change the lot of the poor tribal and in that sense, the demand for a new state could not have been the demand of the tribal masses. Moreover, Chaube seems to believe that the Assamese people and the Hillmen did not have equal status. But it is difficult to understand as to how an ordinary Assamese was better off than an ordinary Hillman. Actually, this desire for an equal status seems to reflect the frustration of the educated elite of the Hills vis-a-vis the Assamese elite.

An APHLC delegation met the Prime Minister on 24 November, 1960. Capt. Sangma raised the language issue in the meeting. The Prime Minister assured Sangma that there was no need to be apprehensive that Assamese would be imposed on the tribals. The Prime Minister, however, opposed the proposal for a separate state for the hill areas on the ground that the entire financial burden of the Hill State would fall on the Government of India; that the creation of separate state would affect the development of the hill areas; and that the available resources could be better utilized for development work.[20]

The delegation met the Prime Minister again on 26 December, 1960. At this meeting, the Prime Minister said that the only satisfactory solution to the problem was to give the tribals full authority in internal matters and complete control over expenditures and freedom in regard to the language they would like to have.[21] Nehru offered the Scottish pattern of government for the Hills. The highlight of the scheme was the constitution of a committee in the Legislative Assembly of Assam comprising all MLAs from the Hills to examine the legislative proposals for the hill areas.[22] The APHLC in its Fourth Session at Shillong (April 5-7, 1961) rejected the proposal since it did 'not solve the basic problems'[23] and resolved to boycott the 1962 elections. The APHLC reiterated its demand for the creation of a separate Hill State and sent a delegation to Delhi which met the Prime Minister on 27 May, 1961. The Prime Minister suggested that the entire matter must be referred to a commission for enquiry and report. The delegation did not agree to this unless the language problem was included in its terms of reference. Thus, the talks eventually failed.[24]

While the APHLC rejected the Scottish Plan, it was accepted by the District Congress Committees. They dissociated themselves from the APHLC and made it plain to the latter that they would contest the third general election on the issue of Scottish Plan. The APHLC was, therefore, compelled to revise its decision. It authorized the Council of Action to take final decision as regards the boycott of elections. The Council which met at Shillong on October 6, 1961, resolved to contest the third general election. The APHLC set up 15 candidates for the election and won 11 seats. Even after this spectacular electoral victory, the dream of a hill state remained unfulfilled. The APHLC carried on agitation, organization and education of the electorate in favour of the Hill State.[25] Having secured a popular mandate for its programmes, the APHLC could now embark upon bolder steps to achieve its ultimate objective.

There was a crack in the party in the second half of 1963. The Mizo Union adopted a rebellious stand towards the APHLC. The Mizos felt that their individuality would be lost by joining the Khasis and the Garos. In these circumstances, the APHLC met the Prime Minister on 10 June, 1963. The result was the emergence of the Nehru Plan which contemplated that the hill areas of Assam must remain within the State of Assam, enjoying ninety nine percent autonomy of a state. There should be a Cabinet Minister in charge of the administration of the hill areas.[26] Nehru clarified that the Hill Minister would have to act according to the norms of the Cabinet Government and

> *"any legislation dealing with the hill areas will, as a matter of convention, have to be approved by their representatives who can certainly initiate legislations also. Such new legislation will be considered by the whole Cabinet. But in so far as it deals with the hill areas only, the views of the hill areas' representatives will have special importance".*[21]

On April 2, 1964, the APHLC member of Lok Sabha, G.G. Swell, had another talk with Nehru on the report of which the APHLC assumed that Nehru had agreed :

(i) that the Prime Minister's Plan of full autonomy and his other assurances be fully implemented both in letter and spirit;

(ii) that the maximum number of subjects be transferred to the hill administration; and

iii) that increased representation be given to the Autonomous Districts both in the State Legislature and Parliament.[29]

The State Government of Assam, the Chief Minister and the Congress opposed the Nehru Plan on the ground that the Plan would affect the democratic form of Government; it would undermine its unity and integrity; it would affect the functioning of the Cabinet as a team with collective responsibility to the State Legislature; it would affect even the unity and integrity of the State; and it would sow the seeds of disruption.[29] In other words, the ruling party of Assam perceived a threat to its authority if the Nehru Plan was adopted and hence resisted the move.

On February 12, 1964, Nehru had told Swell that the whole scheme of autonomy "was subject to a Commission being appointed to consider the whole thing".[30] The proposed Commission was appointed on 16 March 1965 under the Chairmanship of Pataskar. The APHLC extended full cooperation to the Commission which, however, proposed 'no basic change' in the Sixth Schedule.[31] The APHLC was greatly disappointed with the recommendations of the Commission and rejected them raising the demand for a separate Hill State again. Nevertheless, most of the all-India parties welcomed the Commission's recommendations. The APHLC now prepared itself for a fresh round of battle and resolved upon a boycott of the 1967 elections.[32]

Mrs. Indira Gandhi could not afford a boycott of election in a sensitive area of India shortly after her assumption of the Prime Minister's Office. On 27

December 1966, she visited Shillong. The APHLC presented a memorandum demanding a separate Hill State at a mammoth meeting. The Prime Minister replied in general terms that there should be some reorganization which would give dignity and status to the hill people and that this should be done as early as possible. This significant statement was followed by a historic announcement by the Government of India on 13 January, 1967 to reorganize the State of Assam on the basis of a federal structure conferring upon the hill areas equal status with the rest of the State of Assam. Under the arrangement, a limited number of essential subjects of common interest would be assigned to the regional federation leaving the rest of the state functions to the federal units which would have their own legislatures, council of ministers etc.[33]

While these efforts to resolve the problem arising out of the demand for a separate hill state were being made, the CPI began to respond to the problem. In a memorandum to the Union Home Minister, Shri Y. B. Chavan, on Monday 20, 1967, at Gauhati, the Assam State Council, Communist Party of India, stated,

> "The alien Imperialist rulers of the country pursued a policy of keeping the tribal people of the Hills of Assam economically, socially, culturally and politically dwarfed deliberately retarding the normal process of developments of these people. This was quite in keeping with the

Imperialist plan of perpetuating their exploitation and domination of our country ,...".[34]

Thus, guided by its own ideology, the CPI tried to understand the issue in its wider socio-economic context. As the Assam State Executive Committee of the CPI pointed out, the problem of the hills people was basically a problem of their regeneration. The hills people wanted full opportunities for self-expression and for shaping their future freely within the great family of Indian Union. The CPI viewed these urges with profound sympathy and felt that the fulfillment of such genuine aspirations had now become even more urgent to promote integrity of the nation and prosperity of the region.[35] It is interesting to note that unlike the APHLC and the Congress, it did not look at the problem merely from the point of view of the 'development' of the people of the area, but took the question of national integration also into consideration.

With the dawn of Independence, the CPI memorandum stated, it was expected that the new government that came into power would make a serious assessment of the various pressing problems of the tribal people and evolve a new policy that would meet the aspirations of the people and bring them closer with the mainstream of Indian life. The CPI, however, noted with regret that the Congress Government, far from adopting a policy in the above mentioned direction, pursued a policy which was hardly different from that of the alien rulers.

Consequently, the 20-year long Congress rule had not been able to draw the masses of people of the hills of Assam nearer to their counterpart in the plains of the State.[36] The CPI, therefore, felt that the accumulated discontent of the peoples of the Hills areas was largely the creation of the Congress rule. The Congress regime had never taken kindly to the legitimate urges and aspirations of the Hills people and indeed some of its policies and actions only aggravated mistrust and frustration. Thus, the Hills people had been driven to the conclusion through twenty years of Congress rule that unless certain drastic democratic changes were made by reorganizing the State of Assam, their urges were not going to be fulfilled. According to the CPI, the acts of omission and commission of the Congress Governments had contributed to the growth of tensions and conflicts and disruptive tendencies in the hills.[37]

The Assam State Council of the CPI in its memorandum to Chavan expressed the opinion that by pursuing a narrow, sectarian policy with a scarcely hidden domineering outlook, the Congress Government, during 20 years of its rule, far from helping the process of emotional integration, had only helped the forces of disintegration. Little care was taken to develop the State, both the Hills and the Plains, in order to put the entire State on an even footing economically, politically or culturally, ensuring full flowering of the human and natural resources available in the region.[38] The CPI regretted that "Had the Congress Government pursued a policy of balanced development of both the Hills and the Plains of the State with an accelerated pace, the forces of integration might have been strengthened and the present situation might have been averted".[39]

The CPI Memorandum went on to add that along with the advance of literacy and education, an urge had grown among the tribal people for a rapid development of their economy, enrichment of their language and culture and social life. Under the impact of the operation of money economy and the capitalist system that had penetrated into the tribal socio-economic life of the region, the tribal socio-economic structure had been corroded; but a new socio-economic structure that could meet the newly awakened aspirations of the tribal people had not emerged because of the essentially erroneous policy pursued by the Congress Government. Nevertheless, the tribal dialects had been maturing into languages, with a system of Grammar, and the distinct tribes in their respective geographical regions had been emerging as small, but distinct nationalities. The memorandum pointed out that the genuine urge of these emerging nationalities to grow as distinct entities was sought to be exploited by certain reactionary elements, both within and without the tribal societies for the purpose of disintegration and discupation.[40] The Memorandum clearly reflects the CPI's appreciation of genuine aspirations and sensitivities of the hill tribes as well as a willingness to solve their problems within the framework of the communist ideology.

The Memorandum further pointed out that faced with this situation in the course of the last several years, the Government tried in vain to offer some solution to this problem, without any attempt to go deep into it and the result was the various proposals such as the Scottish Pattern of Autonomy, Nehru Plan of Autonomy and the like. But all these superficial, unscientific propositions lacked any basic appraisal of the real nature of the problem and met with failure.[41]

The CPI condemned the Congress Government's bungling on the issue by giving certain assurances to the Hill leaders without even consulting the representatives of the different regions concerned except a few chosen Congress leaders. The Assam State Executive Committee of the CPI warned the Government that the situation had reached a stage when any further drift or any attempts to bypass or distort the real situation seemed fraught with serious dangers. Under the circumstances, the CPI urged for forthright principled democratic solutions, to evolve with all right-minded people called upon to apply their minds. Only thus could the lasting solutions to the long deferred problems be found in the interest of both the Hills and the Plains people, according to the CPI. This was how this strategically important region of India with its great potentiality, the CPI contended, could be freed from tension and turmoil, which was utilized by forces inimical to India.[42]

The State Executive Committee of the CPI regretted the proposal of the Union Home Ministry for the creation of the so-called federal structure in the name of reorganization. Having regard to the realities of the situation, the creation of a federal structure, as envisaged by the Government of India, would, according to the CPI, offer no democratic solution at all. If such a federation was imposed, it would create further complications and keep the tensions and conflicts alive, the CPI predicted.[43] In its memorandum to the Union Home Minister, the CPI expressed its apprehension that the proposed super-state over two or more states would neither ensure the unity and integrity of the people of the Hills and the Plains of the present State of Assam, nor would it guarantee any rapid development of the region. The CPI was of the opinion that the uneven development of the region which had bred suspicion, distrust and prejudice and engendered conflicts would not be removed by this scheme and consequently, the forces of disintegration would find a suitable ground to operate here under the proposed scheme of reorganization of the State. The CPI also felt that the proposed Federation would reduce the status of Assam as a State.[44] The CPI also rejected the notion of a composite Hill State, comprising the hills of Assam because in its view, individual problems of each Hill could not be lumped up on account of the uneven socio-economic, linguistic and cultural development of the different Hills. Instead, the CPI felt, such a state would, in no distant future, face the same conflict as vitiated the then composite state of Assam.[45]

Though the CPI rejected the ill-conceived proposal of the Union Home Ministry for the creation of a federal structure, it reiterated at the same time that it would always be prepared to take counsel with all others in working out correct democratic solutions and not leave matters to be decided by the Central Government in an arbitrary and undemocratic manner.[46]

With these objectives in view, the Assam State Executive Committee of the CPI placed before the people the following basic proposals :

"1. In view of the demands for separate states which have already come up from some hills areas, the hills peoples concerned should be granted separate statehood, each of the hill tribes having its own state. It will, however, be open to them, for more than one such hills peoples, if they so desire, to unite and constitute a single state.

2. After the present Assam State is so reorganized, the newly created hills states may work out and arrange their relations with the State of Assam through mutual consultations and mutual consent".[47]

The CPI recommended in its memorandum to Chavan that,

"... each of the Hill peoples, namely, the Mizos, the Garos, the Khasis etc. should be granted full autonomy within their respective distinct region, with the right to constitute them into Union Territory, if any one of them so desire, with clear provision to remain, out of their own volition, within the State of Assam as Autonomous region".[48]

In the event of any one or more of the Hills opting out of the State of Assam after acquiring Autonomy, the CPI suggested that there should be a coordinating body without any superseding power, for the purpose of executing certain common plans and projects without imposing a superstructure of a Federation. That, in the opinion of the CPI, would meet the requirements of the region.[49]

The Assam State Executive Committee of the CPI was confident that after reorganization, which was in the interest of the peoples of both hills and plains, the State of Assam with its population of more than one crore, with its abundant resources in oil, tea, forest, land etc. would not only remain viable, but also could be developed immensely by necessary economic and other democratic measures for the well-being and advancement of its people, so ruthlessly exploited by the foreign and Indian monopolists thus far.[50]

The CPI, however, felt that,

"... the best interest of both the Hills and the Plains will be served by an integrated Assam.

> *But we do not subscribe to the views of those who would try to achieve that integration even by applying force on the Hills. Such a policy of forced integration may sound heroic. But this is not only undemocratic, but is also damaging to the interest of the country as a whole".*[51]

Nevertheless, the CPI believed that by removing the causes of mutual suspicion, distrust and prejudice that had been accumulating for all these years, the ground would be paved for genuine mutual cooperation, unity and emotional integration of both the Hills and the Plains of the region. Even if some Hills opted out of Assam as a result of the acceptance and implementation of the above mentioned recommendation, the CPI visualized that there would be genuine unity in the days to come, out of the needs and experience of real life and that unity would have a more lasting ground to stand. Hence, the CPI proposed that the Federation idea should be dropped altogether and the solution of the problem should be attempted on the above mentioned scientific basis.[52]

The CPI thus rejected the idea of an integrated Assam that could be achieved only by applying force on the recalcitrant people of the hills. The party stood for emotional integration of the hills and the plains and that alone in its view could guarantee peace, unity, stability and prosperity of the region in the long run. The CPI also approved the existence of a number of Autonomous regions within the State of Assam. The party did not even object to one or more of these units opting out of Assam. It only suggested that in such a case, there should be a co-coordinating body for the purpose of executing common plans and projects. It thus appears that the CPI had a very liberal approach towards the urges of autonomy and statehood voiced by the hills.

Now, whatever apprehensions the CPI might have had regarding the federal proposal, the APHLC welcomed it and decided to participate in the committee composed of representatives of the Government of India, the Government of Assam and the APHLC to be set up to work out the details of the proposed scheme subject to the condition that in the federal structure, the hill state unit should have equal voice and status with the units comprising the remaining State of Assam. However, there was tremendous opposition to the federal plan from a fraction in the Assam Provincial Congress Committee (APCC) opposed to Chaliha, the then Chief Minister of Assam. Hence, the Government did not constitute the Committee to work out the details of the federal scheme. Rather, it called for a joint discussion in Delhi on 7 July, 1967. During the discussion, a Committee, known as the Mehta Committee, was appointed on 8 July consisting of the representatives of the various political parties of the plains and the APHLC, to make an effort to reach an agreed solution for the reorganization of Assam.[53] The APHLC boycotted the Commission which opposed the federal idea and recommended greater autonomy for the hills areas separately. Naturally, the APHLC rejected the Mehta Commission Plan, resigned all the seats it held in the Khasi and the Garo Hills, on May 25, 1968, and started a non-violent Satyagraha on September 10, 1968. On September 11, the Government of India produced the Autonomous State plan for the Garo Hills and the United Khasi-Jaintia Hills Districts. The Mikir and the North Cachar Hills Districts were given the option to join the Autonomous State, if they so decided, in their District Councils, by two-thirds of their strengths. Overwhelmingly, the two District Councils chose to stay with Assam.[54]

This gives an estimate of the APHLC's loss. In a memorandum to the Prime Minister, in early 1961, the APHLC first mentioned 'a state within a state'[55] comprising all the Assam Hills. Meghalaya was set up as a 'state within a state', but much smaller that what it could be in 1961. Full statehood was promised later, but not for all the hills together. On the credit side, the APHLC's record is indeed noteworthy. For the first time in India, a major political demand was fulfilled without practically any violence and by means of sheer organizing ability and public relations.[56]

Following the 22nd Amendment of the Indian Constitution, on December 24, 1969, Parliament created history by passing the Assam Reorganization (Meghalaya) Bill[57] simultaneously in the two Houses in order to create 'an Autonomous State to be known as "Meghalaya" within the State of Assam' comprising the United Khasi-Jaintia Hills District and the Garo Hills District as defined in the Sixth Schedule.[58]

Now, the APHLC's acceptance of the Autonomous State Plan brought into existence intra-party conflict. The extremists who were opposed to the formation of Autonomous State left the APHLC and formed the Hill State People's Democratic Party. To counteract the influence gained by them in certain areas, the APHLC requested the Prime Minister on 3 September, 1970, to declare Meghalaya a full-fledged State. On 10 November, the Prime Minister informed the Lok Sabha that the Government had decided to accept in principle the Meghalaya demand for statehood. On 21 January, 1972, the Prime Minister inaugurated the State of Meghalaya.[59]

It may be noted that the CPI was the first national party to welcome and support the formation of Meghalaya so that the tribal people of Meghalaya might develop their way of life in accordance with their tradition and culture.[60] The CPI declared,

> *"The status of full statehood to Meghalaya has been welcome by the people of the Autonomous State and the Communist Party of India shares the joy of the people. This will enable the masses of people here to participate directly in evolving policies and executing them for the urgently needed social, economic and political upliftments of the people in keeping with the democratic*

> *tradition of the Khasi, the Jaintia and the Garo societies....*"[61]

If, however, we look at the demand for statehood in terms of the aspirations of the emerging tribal elite, we may be able to make some observations regarding the impact of the CPI's stand on this new social force while discussing various perspectives related to this issue. Bani Prasanna Misra refers to the theory that characterizes the political activities among the tribals as falling in the general category of manifestations of 'sub-nationalism' assuming that these movements are essentially based on the economic and political interests of the rising elite who wish to monopolize their dominance over a bonded region and mobilize the relatively passive tribal and peasant masses to fulfill their limited class aspirations.[62] Misra also mentions about the theory according to which sub-nationalism is a by-product of social disorganization when in a welfare state, the gulf between the more developed regions and the less developed regions tends to increase. For Roy Burman, most of the tribal communities of north-east India are passing through phases of infra-nationalism (Modernization to avail of the benefits of advanced technology) or sub-nationalism.[63] While discussing the theory of sub-nationalism, Misra refers to another view implying that the unequal economic development of the hills and the plains areas accentuates political activities in the hill areas of northeast. He felt that the middle class among the tribals are the leaders of the sub-national movement who want equality of opportunity in respect of employment and enterprise and consequently of political status.[64] By citing the triumph that the Khasi Middle Class, particularly the group led by Nichols Roy seemed to have gained over the Chiefs and their allies in the post-independence period, P. N. Dutta observed that as a volatile and ambitious class with division in its ranks, it was not likely to remain content with the rights and powers obtained by the Sixth Schedule. His assumption was that having once tasted the heady wine of power, this middle class might develop appetite for more for what it considered to be interests of the tribe.[65] B.B. Dutta describes the middle class in Meghalaya as the top class which is playing the role of a progressive force.[66] As S.K. Chaube points out, the only avenues open to this middle class were service and professions. The professions were overcrowded and the only source of service in the hills was government. As government was viewed as the chief source of employment, statehood and growth of administration could absorb a part of the pressure.[67] Though social scientists do not seem to agree on the main causes for the demand of statehood, all the arguments mentioned above seem to point to the fact that their demand was directly connected with the aspirations of the emerging tribal elite. As the CPI failed to support the hill state demand unequivocally in the initial stages, it seems to have lost considerable political mileage because the emerging elite happens to be the most dominant political force in the K & J Hills. This failure can be understood only in terms of the interest of the Assamese educated elite and the emerging middle class. The CPI's support for an integrated Assam with safeguards to the hills people was not likely to suit the requirements of these new elite groups among the tribals, who were not content with the existing safeguards, but were eager to share political power.

References

1. Shibanikinkar Chaube, *Hill Politics in North-East India,* (Calcutta, 1973), p. 107.
2. R. Reid, *Years of Change in Bengal and Assam* (London, 1966), p. 110. Also Major A. G. McCall, *Lushai Chrysalis* (London, 1949), p. 241.
3. Verrier Elwyn, *Nagaland* (Shillong, 1961), pp. 51-52.
4. Amalendu Guha, *Planter Raj to Swaraj, Freedom Struggle and Electoral Politics in Assam 1826-1947* (New Delhi, 1977), p. 324.
5. *Ibid.,* p. 322.
6. *Ibid.,* pp. 322-323.
7. V. Venkata Rao, *A Century of Tribal Politics in North East India (1874-1974),* (New Delhi, 1976), pp. 336-367.
8. Memorandum to the States Reorganization Commission submitted by the Hills people of the Autonomous Districts (of Assam), Shillong, 1954; proceedings of the Chief Executive Member' meeting in Appendix 'A'.
9. Shibanikinkar Chaube, *op.cit.,* p. 112.

10. *The Report of the States Reorganization Commission,* Delhi, 1955, p. 188.
11. Shri B. B. Lyngdoh's notes for Discussion with the P.M., 28th August, 1955.
12. For details, see Susmita Sen Gupta, *Regionalism in Meghalaya* (New Delhi, 2005), pp. 69-72.
13. Resolution No. 1(a), passed at the Aizawl Conference 'unanimously'—obtained by S. K. Chaube from Shri B. B. Lyngdoh.
14. Chaube, *op.cit.,* pp. 115-116.
15. V. V. Rao, *op.cit.,* p. 365.
16. Chaube, *op. cit.,* pp. 117-118.
17. *Ibid.,* pp. 118 and 120.
18. V. V. Rao, *op.cit.,* p. 366.
19. Chaube, *op.cit.,* pp. 122-123.
20. V. V. Rao, *op.cit.,* pp. 370-371.
21. *Ibid.,* pp. 372-373.
22. Chaube, *op.cit.,* pp. 124 and 138.
23. APHLC, Memorandum to the Commission on the Hill Areas of Assam Submitted by the All Party Hill Leaders' Conference, Appendix 'D'.
24. V. V. Rao, *op.cit.,* pp. 377-378.
25. *Ibid.,* pp. 378-379.
26. *Ibid.,* pp. 381-383.
27. Quoted in the *Report of the Commission on the Hill Areas of Assam,* (Delhi, 1966, p. 169) from Nehru's letter to Secretary, APHLC, dated February 19, 1961.

28. APHLC's Memorandum, Appendix 'N'.
29. V. V. Rao, *op.cit.,* p. 385.
30. Quoted by the Commission on Hill Areas, *Report,* p. 161.
31. *Ibid.,* p. 127.
32. Chaube, *op.cit.,* p. 126.
33. V. V. Rao, *op.cit.,* pp. 414-415.
34. CPI Memorandum to Y. V. Chavan published in *Shillong Observer,* June 1, 1967, Vol. IX, No. 4, p. 3.
35. *Shillong Observer,* August 1, 1967, Vol. IX, No. 8, p. 1.
36. CPI Memorandum, *op.cit.,* p. 3.
37. *Shillong Observer, op.cit.,* p. 1.
38. CPI Memorandum, *op.cit.,* p. 3.
39. *Loc.cit.*
40. *Loc.cit.*
41. *Loc.cit.*
42. *Shillong Observer, op. cit.,* p. 5.
43. *Loc.cit.*
44. CPI Memorandum, *op.cit.,* p. 3.
45. *Loc.cit.*
46. *Shillong Observer, op.cit.,* p. 5.
47. *Loc.cit.*
48. CPI Memorandum, *op.cit.,* p. 3.
49. *Loc. cit.*
50. *Shillong Observer, op.cit.,* p. 5.

51. CPI Memorandum, *op. cit.*, p. 3.
52. *Loc.cit.*
53. V. V. Rao, *op.cit.*, pp. 416-424.
54. S. K. Chaube, *op.cit.*, p. 127.
55. Quoted in the *Pataskar Report,* p. 163.
56. S. K. Chaube, *op.cit.*, p. 127.
57. *Act No. 55 of 1969.* It obtained the President's assent on December 29, 1969, vide *The Gazette of India, Extraordinary, Part II, Section II.*
58. Paragraph 20, *Sixth Schedule.*
59. V. V. Rao, *op.cit.*, p. 451.
60. *CPI on Burning Problems of Meghalaya* issued by the Meghalaya State Council, CPI, October 20, 1983, p. 5.
61. *Meghalaya's Road to Prosperity: Draft Programme of the Meghalaya Coordination Committee of the CPI,* p. 1.
62. Bani Prasanna Misra, "Society and Politics in the Hill Areas of North East India" in B. Datta Ray (ed.), *The Emergence and Role of Middle Class in North-East India,* (New Delhi, 1983), pp. 13-14.
63. *Ibid.*, p. 14.
64. *Loc.cit.*
65. P. N. Dutta, 'The Emergence and Role of Middle Class in the Khasi Jaintia Hills 1824-1950' in B. Datta Ray (ed.), *op.cit.* p. 145. It may be noted in this context that there has been a major debate on whether there has emerged a middle class in the hills in general and Khasi, Jaintia and Garo Hills

in particular. The author has argued against the application of the term 'middle class' in the context of the said hill areas. For details, See Susmita Sen Gupta, *Regionalism in Meghalaya, op.cit.,* p. 35.

66. B. B. Dutta, 'Emergence and Role of Middle Class in Meghalaya' in B. Datta Ray (ed.), *op.cit.,* p. 179.

67. See S. K. Chaube, 'The Middle Class in the North-East Indian Hills: Retrospects and Prospects', in B. Datta Ray (ed.), *op.cit.,* pp. 45-46.

3

CPI and Its Front Organizations in Meghalaya

With the creation of Meghalaya, the Khasi, the Jaintia and the Garo peoples' dream of Statehood was realized. The Meghalaya Coordination Committee of the CPI was formed after the inauguration of the Autonomous State of Meghalaya to carry on the activities of the party in the newly born State. The CPI set for itself a variety of challenging tasks in the emerging socio-political milieu. Now, the most important auxiliaries of a Communist Party are its mass organizations, which are the source of the Party's main political power; it is through them that the Communists endeavour to mobilize the full might of the working class and its allies for the tasks of the revolution.[1] In 1924, Stalin defined the role of the mass organizations and their relationship to the Party as follows :

> *The Party is not the only organization of the working class. The proletariat has also a number of other organizations, without which it cannot properly wage the struggle against capital: trade unions, cooperatives societies, factory and works organizations.... All these organizations, under*

certain conditions, are absolutely necessary for the working class.[2]

To the CPI, the most important mass organizations have been those of the workers, peasants, students and women. Among these, the trade-union organizations have been the source of the Party's greatest political power.[3]

Just as the mass organizations serve as "transmission belts" between the Party and the working class at large, so "front" organizations link the party to "progressive" elements of other classes. The Communist fronts in India can be grouped into three categories - first, the international issue fronts, second, the professional fronts and finally, the regional fronts.[4] The CPI in Meghalaya has a number of front organizations which carry on activities in various fields on behalf of the parent organization. Our attempt in this chapter will be to examine the role played by these fronts of the CPI as agents of radical mass-mobilization.

The most prominent among the mass organizations of the CPI in Meghalaya are Students' Federation and Youth Federation, National Federation of Indian Women (Mahila Samity) and units of All-India Kisan Sabha and All India Trade Union Congress. Apart from these organizations, which are affiliated to the CPI, there are the All India Peace and Solidarity Organization and the Indo-Soviet Cultural Society where the Communists play an active role along with other political parties.

Students' Federation and Youth Federation

Towards the end of the First World War, students began to be an important factor in Indian politics, and Gandhi's civil-disobedience campaigns drew thousands away from their studies to participate in the struggle for independence. In August, 1936, the first All-India Student Conference was held in Lucknow on the initiative of the United Provinces Student Federation and from this meeting the All India Students' Federation later emerged.[5] A statement was adopted in the conference which declared that one of the aims and objects of the organization was 'to prepare the students for citizenship, in order to take their due share in the struggle for complete national freedom, by arousing their political, social and economic consciousness".[6] Three months after the meeting in Lucknow, a second conference was held in Lahore which adopted a constitution and the All-India Students' Federation was formally launched. Although there is no evidence in the available CPI literature that the Communists had selected the student movement as an important target for penetration, according to Overstreet and Windmiller, there are indications that by 1938, a substantial percentage of the Federation was pro-Soviet, if not pro-Communist.[7] Many of the leaders of the AISF joined the CPI while students. Others joined the Party after ceasing to be active in the student movement. It thus appears that the AISF is both a recruiting and a training organization for the CPI. On international questions, the AISF has taken a pro-Soviet, anti-American line, and on domestic issues, it has attempted to become a militant champion of political reform and of better facilities for students. It has been active in the many student strikes that have taken place in India since independence. Overstreet and Windmiller, however, feel that it would be a mistake to place the blame for student unrest on the AISF. The causes according to them are much more complex, and the AISF has, apparently, only tried to capitalize on existing grievances.[9]

Let us focus our attention back on the Meghalaya context. Shillong Students' Federation was formed in 1938 with Sailen Neogy as Secretary. This was preceded by the radicalization of the youth and students of Shillong as a result of the visits to Shillong by a number of All India leaders with left leanings. In 1939-40, Barin Dutta, a member of the Sylhet Communist Party group, came to Shillong while being underground and indoctrinated a section of youth and students of Shillong through party classes on Marxism-Leninism. Jyotirmoy Nandy also contributed to the rearing up of this group of party sympathizers.[10]

The Shillong Students' Federation and Girls Students' Committee under the leadership of Arun Roy, Prafulla Misra, M. Bhattacharya, Anjali Das, Kanika Ghosh, Arati Das and others participated in the post-war revolutionary upsurge like INA Day, Rashid Ali Day, Anti-Grouping Scheme Day and

Vietnam Day.[11] The Students' Federation was able to establish rapport with the hills students in various colleges of Assam and Calcutta. It helped the hill students to organize the Hill Students' Federation with T. Aliba Imti Ao, a Naga student, as its secretary.[12]

All India Students' Federation was formally inaugurated in Shillong in 1968. At that time, there were thirty-five active members of the AISF, although officially there were as many as 200 members. Jaid Singh was the General Secretary of the AISF. Later on, Mr. Paswa was elected General Secretary who held that post till 1970. Miss Jaya Dutta, a student of Lady Keane College, was the President of the Students' Federation. There were twenty-one executive members who used to meet once in three months. The strength of the Students' Federation was limited in and around Shillong. The funds of the AISF came mainly from members' subscriptions. The AISF did not have any publications during the initial years of its formation.[13]

Some of the issues before the Students' Federation were - free education upto Degree level, cheap rate of text books, unemployment, opening up of industry, cultural upliftment of the people etc. Apart from these, the AISF demanded the introduction of the Kothari Commission recommendations in the Secondary Schools and also the introduction of education based on scientific method. The Meghalaya Unit of the Students' Federation organized food movement, oil refinery movement etc. In this connection, meetings were held and a procession was organized in front of the Secretariat and the State Library. However, the dearth of active members stood in the way of the AISF's growth in Meghalaya.[14]

Now, after Meghalaya was created as a full-fledged State, Meghalaya State Council of All India Students' Federation was formally organized in 1972. The growth of the Students' Federation in Meghalaya has been closely linked with that of the Communist Party itself. The AISF has not brought the mass of the students under its banner. The Students' Federation is still in its formative stage in Meghalaya. It has not been able to build particularly strong organizations anywhere in Meghalaya. In some areas of Garo Hills, however, notably in Mahendraganj, where Bengalis constitute a compact ethnic group, the AISF has a good nucleus. During the early years of its formation, a number of Khasi Students joined the Students' Federation. But the ethnic crisis and the communal tension that followed it, led to substantial erosion in the strength of the AISF. In Shillong, some Khasi boys had joined the AISF. Local Bengalis, however, do not seem to be particularly interested in associating themselves with the Students' Federation.[15]

During the AISF conference held in 1986, Ranjit Kar was the General Secretary. Later, a Khasi youth from Nongstoin, Lawrence Nongbri,was given an opportunity to run the affairs of the Students' Federation. Meanwhile, a joint conference of the Students' Federation and the Youth Federation was planned to be held in May-June, 1988, in which Mr. Ranjit Kar anticipated a good participation. Miss Jaya Dutta, a student of Lady Keane College and Mr. Lamare from Jowai, are among those who were in-charge of the Meghalaya Students' Federation earlier. At present, there are eight executive members of the AISF in Meghalaya. However, the executive does not meet very often. Efforts are being made to give an organized shape to the AISF.[16]

The Meghalaya unit of Students' Federation depends for its funds on donation from members. The AISF has no regular publications in Meghalaya. But it has published some leaflets from time to time. A leaflet was published, for example, in connection with a public meeting against war held at Opera Hall on 25th February, 1984.[17] Jokendra Lanong, Secretary, Shillong City Council, CPI, Ranjit Kar, General Secretary, Meghalaya State Council, AISF, R. Das, Secretary, Shillong Local Committee, CPI (M), K. P. Sarma, Secretary, Democratic Youth Federation, Shillong branch and Samudra Gupta, Secretary, Progressive Youth Association, jointly invited the citizens of Shillong to attend the public meeting to voice their protest against war for World Peace. Another leaflet was published on the occasion of a joint conference of the North Eastern State Units of All India Youth Federation and All India Students' Federation held at Shillong on December 13 and 14, 1986, in which Dr. B. N. Roy Chowdhury, Convener, Reception Committee, appealed to the public to contribute generously for the success of the conference. Apart from these, an appeal was issued through a leaflet to all sections of the public to extend their co-operation for the success of a three-day state level Youth Festival observed in Shillong from 6th to 8th July, 1978, in honour of the XIth World Youth Festival held at Havana, Cuba. The Festival included sports, debate, seminar and a cultural function was held at State Central Library Auditorium on the concluding day. Certificates were issued by the Meghalaya State Preparatory Committee (for XIIth World Festival of Youth and Students, Moscow, 1985) Shillong, to those officials and competitors who participated in the Festival and came out with outstanding performance.[18] Recently, the AISF decided to publish a Khasi paper. But the plan has not materialized as yet.

In Meghalaya today, ethnic issues have assumed a lot of significance. But the AISF could not take any clear-cut stand on such issues. Meghalaya AISF leaders maintain that the activities of the Students' Federation received a setback after the ethnic disturbances of 1979. But following some improvement in the situation, the activists of the AISF have been recently addressing street meetings on price-rise etc.[19] But in real terms, these efforts did not have much significance so much so that the small meetings that they organized did not find any mention even in the local press.

Ranjit Kar, the former General Secretary of the Meghalaya AISF, points out the importance of the appeal of ethnic identity in Meghalaya leading to the formation of organizations based on ethnic lines, viz., Khasi Students' Union, Garo Students' Union etc. All the students belonging to a particular organization may not owe their allegiance to a definite ideology, but the bond of ethnic identity holds them together. Thus, the student community in Meghalaya is not a unified group due to lack of commitment to common goals. It is, therefore, difficult for the Students' Federation to organize the student community in Meghalaya on the basis of any ideological commitments.[20] Moreover, as in Meghalaya, the proletariat has not grown due to the slow process of industrialization, there is lack of class consciousness among the students which stands in the way of mobilizing them. In Meghalaya, the unemployment problem being less acute as compared to other states of India, the Students' Federation could not organize the students on the basis of issues like unemployment. In recent years, however, unemployment reached ominous proportions in Meghalaya as in other parts of the country. But the AISF could not capitalize on this issue for purposes of mobilization.

As the growth of the AISF is closely linked to that of the CPI, Ranjit Kar feels that acceptability of the communist ideology may gradually draw more students to the AISF. He claims that the Meghalaya unit of the Students' Federation has been working with the long-term objective of mobilizing the students and youth of the entire North-Eastern region. The AISF has been able to recruit students from other states and by distributing leaflets etc., efforts are being made to popularize socialist ideas among them.[21] It is interesting to note that even Kar does not try to examine why communist ideology is not acceptable among the masses. Obviously, the CPI does not have strong mass organizations in Meghalaya with which to propagate its ideas among the people.

The unit of All India Youth Federation was formed in Meghalaya along with that of AISF in 1972. Even before Meghalaya received the status of full statehood, a branch of the Youth Federation was organized in 1968. At the time of its foundation, the Youth Federation had nineteen members and Late Sushil Goswami, Shibdas Nandy and Umapada Deb were General Secretary, President and Treasurer respectively. Since 1970, Umapada Deb functioned as the General Secretary. There were seven executive members who used to meet once in three months. The influence of the Youth Federation was limited in and around Shillong at the initial stages and there was dearth of active members among the local people. The issues for which the Youth Federation fought were - unemployment, free education, industrialization, introduction of modern method of agriculture, control of price rise, introduction of job-oriented education etc. Processions and meetings were organized very often on the issues of price rise, unemployment and in connection with the oil refinery movement.[22] In 1971, the Shillong Committee of the CPI along with the Youth Federation and Students' Federation held demonstrations in front of the Deputy Commissioner's Office demanding food and holding of the price line of consumer goods.[23] The Youth Federation organized several youth festivals and since 1973, elected members from the State participated in the World Youth Festivals once in every three or five years.[24]

At present, the AIYF in Meghalaya has about 1,000 members. There is not much scope for expansion of the Youth Federation in Meghalaya because its membership is based on small ethnic groups like Hajongs. The AIYF has comparatively stronger organizations in Garo Hills and in Shillong, there are about forty active members of the Youth Federation. The AIYF has a ten-member executive body which does not meet regularly. There was no General Secretary of the AIYF at the time of the interview. Dr. B. N. Roy Chowdhury was supervising the activities of the organization with the assistance of other members. Thc Youth Federation had taken up issues like Bhopal Gas Tragedy and fought against multinational companies. It campaigned for 'Jail Bharo' and expressed solidarity with the all-India programme of 'job or jail'. The Youth

Federation in Meghalaya has no independent publications of its own. In fact, the AISF and the AIYF cannot be strictly separated as two different organizations because these organizations are very weak in Meghalaya.[25]

All-India Trade Union Congress and its Unit in Meghalaya

The All-India Trade Union Congress, the first national trade union federation, was formed in 1920. The organizers of the AITUC were not Marxist revolutionaries, but bourgeois nationalists with close links with the Indian National Congress, who were motivated by humanitarianism as well as nationalism.[26] When the AITUC held its Second Annual Session in Jharia (Bihar), on November 30, 1921, the Red International of Labour Unions sent its greetings and appealed to the Indian organization "to join in the new great world movement of international solidarity on absolutely equal terms".[27] However, the Indian Communists were slow in gaining a foothold in the trade union movement and according to Overstreet and Windmiller, whatever success they achieved in the beginning, appears to have been due to the efforts of British comrades. As early as 1924, the British Communist Party began organizing Indian seamen who came to British ports.[28] Overstreet and Windmiller suggest on the basis of available evidence that the Communists in India had not engaged in any important trade union activity before the arrival of George Allison in April,

1926.[29] Within a year after his arrival, the Communists were able to report some success in organizing textile workers, railwaymen, municipal workers, dockers, and pressmen, mostly in Bombay.[30]

Communist interest in the AITUC was apparent as early as 1925 when D. R. Thengdi, a Communist sympathizer, who was President at the organization's Bombay meeting, made a speech on class war which irritated the dominant moderate element.[31] By 1927, the Communists began to exert considerable influence in the AITUC. The first real Communist challenge to the moderates came at the Ninth Session in Jharia in December, 1928, when the arrest of a fraternal delegate from the League Against Imperialism led the infuriated delegates to decide in favour of affiliating the AITUC with the League.[32] At the Tenth Annual Session of the AITUC in Nagpur, on November 30, 1929, Jawaharlal Nehru and S. A. Dange were elected President and General Secretary respectively. The Communists also captured other important offices in the organization.[33] After the Nagpur Session, N. M. Joshi and the moderates set up the Indian Trade Union Federation and in 1931, the Communists under S. V. Deshpande and B. T. Ranadive left the AITUC and formed the Red Trade Union Congress. However, the Communists came back into the AITUC in April, 1935 in accordance with their united front policy.[34] During the "Quit India" movement in August, 1942, the imprisonment of most of the nationalist leaders enabled the Communists to gain firm control of the AITUC because they were free to pursue their political activities for supporting the British war effort. When the National Congress leaders failed to break the Communist hold on the AITUC after the war, they set up their own federation in May, 1947, the Indian National Trade Union Congress (INTUC).[35]

After examining the AITUC Constitution, Overstreet and Windmiller observed that of prior importance for the AITUC are the establishment of a Socialist State and the nationalization of the means of production, distribution and exchange, whereas the amelioration of the economic and social conditions of the working classes ranks third among its objectives. They concluded therefore that the primary function of the AITUC is political.[36]

After Meghalaya was born as a full-fledged State, a unit of All India Trade Union Congress was formally inaugurated in 1972. At the time of its formation, Binoy Lahiri was the President and Prafulla Misra was the General Secretary of the AITUC. Dalington Dympep and Robin Rema were Vice-Presidents and representatives from each union affiliated to the AITUC were members of the executive. After Prafulla Misra became the full time party journalist, he had to resign and B. K. Deb Roy became the General Secretary of the AITUC. During the early years of the formation of the AITUC, Meghalaya Jute Mill Workers' Union in Byrnihat,

Khasi Hills Saw Mill Workers' Union, Meghalaya PWD Master Roll Workers' Union, Shillong Municipal Harijan Mazdoor Union, Kumora Limestone Mining Workers' Union and Meghalaya Plywood Workers' Union were affiliated with the AITUC.[37] Meghalaya PWD Master Roll Workers' Union affiliated with the AITUC is composed mostly of casual labourers. It is shocking to note that in India, there are no provisions for leave, medical aid and other benefits for casual workers. Thus many casual labourers are working for as long as thirty years without getting any benefits. AITUC organized these workers some time in 1975-76 mostly in and around Shillong in Khasi Hills. At that time, the daily wage of these labourers was Rs. 3 only. The AITUC started negotiations with the Labour Department. Many officers promised to consider the suggestions given by the AITUC. The AITUC quoted provisions of labour law, e.g., Instrument of Negotiation Act which provides that if a labourer works for six days continuously, he is entitled to a break on the seventh day. After initial resistance, the administration was eventually forced to concede the demand for a day's break. In the matter of raising pay scales, however, the AITUC could not extract any substantial concessions. They demanded that there should be a minimum wages committee to review the position. Ultimately, a committee was set up which proposed to raise the wage from Rs. 3 to Rs. 5. However, even after the introduction of the new rate of daily wages, the union had to fight for receipt of arrears which accumulated in the period during which the Government undertook certain formalities after issuing the order. Prior to the formation of the union, an illegal practice was also in force. Labour supervisors and in some cases overseers used to make an arrangement for appropriating money on a monthly basis after giving appointment to a labourer. The AITUC succeeded in putting an end to this practice. Due to the AITUC'S efforts, the wage of the labourers went up to Rs. 15 per day. But another arbitrary practice of deducting two or three days' pay for one day's absence is still in force. On the whole, however, PWD Master Roll Workers' Union has become an All Meghalaya Union with branches in Jaintia and Garo Hills also. This AITUC affiliated union now has the biggest paid membership. Although Indian National Trade Union Congress also has organized a union which is concentrated in West Garo Hills, it has no paid members as such.

Shillong Municipal Harijan Mazdoor Union is also associated with the AITUC in Meghalaya. This union fought hard for improving the lot of the workers whose pay was a meagre Rs. 100 per month. Now, the workers are treated as Class IV employees of the Government of Meghalaya and are enjoying the corresponding benefits. They are entitled to provident fund and are also availing leave like Class IV employees. At present, the union is fighting for pension and gratuity.[39]

Meghalaya Plywood Workers' Union was also controlled by the AITUC. AITUC leaders alleged that the owner of the Plywood Mill, Jagannath Bawri, as well as the State Government were violating many laws. Though at the time of issuing licences, it was promised that majority of the labourers would be employed out of the indigenous labour force, only casual labourers were ultimately recruited from amongst the tribals. Moreover, pay was very low and there was discrimination of treatment between men and women workers. The AITUC took up with the authorities the issues relating to increase of pay and allowances, regulation of working hours etc. The management sent a representation to the Labour Department. According to AITUC sources, the Labour Department gave a report which went against the interests of the workers. The management also discharged some of the local women organizers. The union took up the matter with the Labour Department, but the management emerged as the winner in this battle with the union.[40] Eventually, most of the organizers either left on their own or were discharged on some plea or the other. Thus, after functioning for nearly two years, the union collapsed.[41]

Meghalaya Jute Mill Workers' Union was also under the control of the AITUC. Initially, the Union could wield some influence. It fought for revision of pay scales etc. and could derive some concessions from the management. But this union also could not be maintained for a long time. After this union was dissolved, there was no union in that mill for quite some time. A union was later formed with a CITU leader from Gauhati as its organizer.[42]

AITUC organized Kumora Limestone Mining Workers' Union during 1976-77. The daily wage of the workers at that time varied between Rs. 4 and Rs. 7 per day, the highest rate being meant for skilled labourers like drillers. AITUC took up with the authorities issues like revision of pay scale, leave rules, working hours, medical aid, contributory provident fund etc. In the matter of revision of pay scales, the Report of the All India Wage Board constituted by the Government of India which was applicable in Meghalaya was not implemented by the management. The Union persuaded the management to implement the Wage Board Report, though the management agreed to do so in phase because of paucity of funds. Before the workers resorted to the first strike, an unskilled labourer's pay was Rs.120 only per month and he was not entitled to dearness allowance or variable dearness allowance. After an agreement was signed between the Union and the management, the unskilled labourer's pay rose to Rs. 400 per month. When the Union was finally disaffiliated from the AITUC, the total emolument of the unskilled worker had gone up to Rs. 750 along with D.A. and V.D.A. He also became entitled to free housing facility, free medical aid and free water and electric supply.[43] But ultimately, this union collapsed as a result of the infiltration by some CPI (M) elements whose radical promises led the workers to believe that AITUC was not capable of achieving anything extraordinary for them. After snatching this union from the AITUC, the CPI (M), too, could not retain its control over it. It was ousted by another group and eventually INTUC stepped in. As Lahiri points out, many trade union leaders of this region tend to underestimate the management in North East India - its experience and understanding of trade union tactics and statistical aspects of management. This interpretation, according to Lahiri, is basically wrong. His long association with the trade union movement in this region enabled him to recognize the truly clever potentialities of the management. AITUC itself, he felt, has fallen a victim to these clever manoeuvrings and as a result, most of the unions formerly affiliated with it, have broken away. Thus, PWD Master Roll Workers' Union and Shillong Municipal Harijan Mazdoor Union are the only two unions controlled by the AITUC in Meghalaya today.[44]

On the 16th of September, 2005, the AITUC organized a procession of over five hundred daily wage labourers to press for their demand for better working conditions in State Government departments and industrial units. It was pointed out by Mr. Dalington Dympep, Secretary, AITUC, Shillong unit, that the daily wage earners are victims of whimsical and arbitrary action of authorities and that there are instances when workers do not get minimum wages according to the law. He also highlighted that the condition of workers employed in the private sector, particularly in the industrial unit in Byrnihat, is worse.[45]

In short, however, it appears that the AITUC has not been able to build up any significant labour movement in Meghalaya. Since immigrant labourers constitute the bulk of the working force in Meghalaya, the tribals do not usually render support to the working class struggles. In the absence of local support, the AITUC cannot be expected to achieve any major breakthrough as far as the trade union movement in Meghalaya is concerned.

All-India Kisan Sabha in Meghalaya

Recognizing the political importance of the Indian peasantry, the Comintern set up a special section of the Krestintern (the Comintern's peasant international) in 1926 to carry on work among Indian peasants. But despite this early interest, the Communists have not been very successful in organizing the 85 percent of the Indian people who earn their livelihood from agriculture.[46] Though N. G. Ranga began to organize a series of peasant conferences, mostly in Andhra since 1923,[47] an all-India peasant movement did not take shape until April, 1936, when the first All-India Kisan Congress was held in Lucknow under the presidency of Swami Sahajananda Saraswathi, a peasant leader from Bihar. A second Congress was held in Faizpur in December, 1936, in which N. G. Ranga and Swami Sahajananda Saraswathi were elected as President and General Secretary respectively with Indulal Yajnik, B. P. L. Bedi and Bankim Mukherhjee as joint secretaries.[48]

Within the Kisan movement, four elements fought for control: the Communists, the Congress Socialists, and two regionally oriented groups led by N. G. Ranga and Swami Sahajananda Saraswathi, respectively. In 1936, the Communists cooperated with Ranga to defeat the Congress Socialists,[49] but lost him in 1941 during the transition from "Imperialist War" to "People's War". As they gained more power in the All India Kisan Sabha (this name was adopted in 1938), the Communists increasingly tended to regard the organization as a subsidiary of the CPI. This irritated both Indulal Yajnik and Swami Saraswathi and eventually both of them left the AIKS. At the end of the war, the Communists found themselves virtually alone in the AIKS. Although the Communists had had some success in organizing local peasant demonstrations, their hold in the countryside had been considerably weakened.[50] Before the Communist peasant leaders had time to erase the odium arising from their opposition to the nationalist movement during the war, the CPI embarked on the militant leftist strategy of the Ranadive period. The resulting police repression practically eliminated the AIKS as a national organization.[51] Overstreet and Windmiller, however, point out that the weakening of the AIKS does not necessarily mean a diminution of Communist influence in rural India. At the same time, they admit that when the Communists parted company with the Socialists, they lost the large rural followings of many Socialist leaders. They also mention CPI's quandary with regard to the landless agricultural workers as one of the factors limiting Communist success among the rural elements. The interests of the landless workers do not coincide with those of the peasantry and there have been no indications in recent years that the Communists have found a way to take advantage of the militancy of agricultural labourers without losing their support among the peasants.[52]

As far as All India Kisan Sabha in Meghalaya is concerned, there is no statewide organization covering the whole of Meghalaya. In Khasi Hills, a Kisan Sabha was formed during 1976-77, called the Farmers' Union.[53] The Farmers' Union is concentrated in Bhoi area of North Khasi Hills. Its organizer- secretary was Orister Syngklie - a State Council member of the CPI. During 1976-78, the Union fought for some agricultural reforms as well as took up some general problems of the area. When the State Government encouraged coffee and tea cultivation in Meghalaya, the Farmers' Union pointed out that the Bhoi area had favourable conditions for the growth of coffee. As the distribution of coffee plants among the peasants began, the Farmers' Union pressed upon the Government that the seeds should be distributed through the Union. Accordingly, the Union held several big meetings in Bhoiryimbong area and about 7,000 plants were distributed among the farmers. The Farmers' Union also fought two battles against illegal occupation of land.[54] At present, however, the Farmers' Union has ceased to be as active as it was before.

In Jaintia Hill and Garo Hills also, Kisan Sabha organizations have been formed which deal mostly with local problems. In Garo Hills, Jatindra Hajong and N. L. Misra were the General Secretaries of the Kisan Sabha. In 1969, a big rally was organized in Tura, which was attended by several thousands of peasants from all parts of Garo Hills. The peasants came with various pressing demands some of which were realized. In 1986 also, a rally was organized in Garo Hills. A conference of the Kisan Sabha was held in April, 1988, in which some burning issues affecting the peasants were discussed.[55]

In a paper entitled "Land and Land Relations in Meghalaya", Lahiri pointed out the presence of a large number of 'Sharecroppers' in Meghalaya. The Land Reform Commission's report for Khasi Hills (1974) showed that many of the landowners took back the land from the sharecroppers and got it cultivated through labourers to prove that they were owner cultivators. Lahiri also pointed out the absence of laws to protect the rights of tenants in Meghalaya. There is concentration of land in the hands of a few non-cultivators. In the absence of laws prohibiting eviction of farmers, eviction of real cultivators of land by the richer section among the tribal people is going on unabated throughout Meghalaya.[56] During the late seventies, the Government of Meghalaya agreed in principle to constitute a Land Reform Commission. The CPI organized a mass signature campaign throughout Meghalaya and held mass meetings to popularize the idea of forming the Land Reform Commission. Demands were made for cadestral survey of land, preparation of records of rights as well as a Census operation of sharecroppers in order to find out how the system was functioning.[57] Some fifteen thousand signatures were procured from the affected peasants of Meghalaya as a whole, most of the peasants being tribals. Having thus generated public opinion in favour of the idea throughout Meghalaya, a memorandum was submitted to the Government by the CPI. The Congress, which was then in the opposition, opposed cadestral survey of land. Moreover, some prominent members of the APHLC demanded the holding of a referendum on the issue. Finally, the Government set up a Land Reform Commission which submitted a report at the end of its two-year term. But since then, no action was taken. During the Sixth Five Year Plan, the Government decided to cadestrally survey 23,000 villages and the necessary finance was earmarked for the purpose. But at the end of the Sixth Plan, Lahiri himself reviewed the situation and found that only 125 villages were cadestrally surveyed, though no maps or record of rights were prepared. Thus, the whole process ended up as an exercise in futility.[58]

Indo-Soviet Cultural Society in Meghalaya

In February, 1952, a group of fellow travellers[59] in Bombay formed a preparatory committee for an Indo-Soviet Festival and Convention to be held in that city the following month, simultaneously with the visit to India of a Soviet delegation led by the Russian writer, Nikolai Tikhonov.[60] The Convention took place on March 14, 1952, and from it emerged the Indo-Soviet Cultural Society (ISCS). Dr. A. V. Baliga, a Bombay Surgeon, was elected President, and S. Venkataraman was made General Secretary.[61] The new organization has attempted to appear non-political. Its journal says :

> *"Our Society and its official journal ISCUS stand wholeheartedly for cultural exchanges, cultural understanding and cultural ties between Soviet Russia and India. As we have already declared we are unconcerned with politics ... ."*.[62]

The techniques by which the Society seeks to promote those aims are :

(a) Holding meetings, lectures, discussions and study circles;

(b) Facilitating exchange of delegations and study tours between India and the USSR;

(c) Staging plays and organizing political symposia and poetry-reading groups;

(d) Arranging exhibitions of art, photography, stamps, manuscripts, etc.;

(e) Organizing reading rooms and libraries;

(f) Assisting persons interested in learning each others' languages;

(g) Arranging the exchange of students, scholars, artists and professors between Indian and Soviet cultural institutions;

(h) Procuring the translation into Indian languages of books and publications relating to Soviet culture;

(i) Publication and distribution of books, journals, etc. relating to Indian and Soviet culture;

(j) Developing pen-friendships; and

(k) Other similar activities in furtherance of the aim of the Society.[63]

By the time of its third National Conference, held in Calcutta in December, 1956, ISCUS was able to report the existence of 42 branches scattered all over India. The total membership of the 21 branches that sent figures to the central headquarters was 7,670.[64]

Meghalaya State Level Committee of Indo-Soviet Cultural Society was formed in 1973. The ISCUS being a very broad forum, all those who have faith in Indo-Soviet friendship are eligible for its membership. Thus, along with CPI, all other political parties in Meghalaya except People's Demand Implementation Convention (PDIC) and even non-partymen like M. Chakravarty were involved in its activities.[65]

In the first conference of ISCUS (Meghalaya) held in 1973, Prafulla Misra of CPI and Jor Manik Syiem were elected General Secretary and President respectively of the Meghalaya State Committee of ISCUS. After the Second Conference held in 1976 (tentatively), Maham Singh of Indian National Congress became the President. P. Misra and M. Chakravarty were elected as General Secretaries. The Third Conference held in 1982 re-elected Maham Singh as President who held that post till his death in 1987. Prafulla Misra continued to be the General Secretary. M. Chakravarty, O. L. Nongtdu and Prof. D. L. Warjri were three other General Secretaries. John Deng Pohrmen (Minister of Education) who was Vice-President of ISCUS succeeded Mr. Maham Singh as President.[66]

According to the Cultural Exchange Agreement signed between Indo-Soviet Cultural Society, National Council, and Soviet India Friendship Society (counterpart of ISCUS), Meghalaya was connected with Tatar Autonomous Republic of former USSR. In accordance with the Agreement, several cultural delegations from Meghalaya visited Tatar Autonomous Soviet Socialist Republic.[67] However, absence of Government approval due to strict rules and regulations regarding foreigners' entry in this area has so far prevented the Meghalaya State Committee of ISCUS from officially entertaining delegations from the erstwhile USSR. The then Chief Minister of Meghalaya, Mr. P. A. Sangma, had reportedly assured ISCUS of Government permission to invite delegations from the USSR and agreed to treat the members of the delegations as State guests. On the basis of this assurance, invitations were sent out by the Meghalaya ISCUS to delegations from the USSR. The Cultural Department of the Soviet Consulate in Calcutta had also offered to extend cooperation in this regard. Chakravarty was expecting an audio-visual publicity van carrying films from Russia in the middle of May 1988 for arranging film shows all over the State.[68]

According to M. Chakravarty, five cultural delegations have so far visited USSR from Meghalaya. These delegations were led by Percylina Marak (who visited USSR as leader of Youth delegates of All-India ISCUS), A. C. Marak, D. D. Lapang, O. L. Nongtdu and Hereford S. Sawian respectively. Chakravarty himself was a member of the delegation led by D. D. Lapang.[69] Prafulla Misra points out that late Maham Singh, B. B. Dutta (former General Secretary of Meghalaya Pradesh Congress Committee (I), Dr. Devika Saikia (Office-bearer, ISCUS) and Robin Rema (CPI leader from Garo Hills) were among those who visited USSR with different cultural delegations from Meghalaya.[70] Prominent persons like D. N. Joshi (ex-MLA), B. K. Roy and Bhaskar Chaudhury (both ex-MLAs) were also associated with the activities of ISCUS.[71]

In late seventies, a Russian cultural troupe (Tadjik) visited Shillong and presented cultural shows in State Central Library. Along with that troupe, pilot cosmonaut Klimik also visited Shillong. A reception was given to them by ISCUS in State Central Library. A reception was also given to Mr. Goldwin, Minister of Heavy Industries, USSR, in his capacity as President of Soviet-India Friendship society, when he visited Shillong.[72] A Russian Ballet Troupe visited Shillong in March, 1988. A reception was accorded to them by ISCUS on March 17.[73]

As to the effectiveness of the Indo-Soviet Cultural Society, Overstreet and Windmiller point out that till 1957, it had been unable to draw into its organization any persons of prominence comparable to those who supported its predecessor, All India Friends of the Soviet Union in 1944, implying that it was not making a great impression on India's ruling elite.[74] As far as the ISCUS in Meghalaya is concerned, however, we find that a number of Ministers, Legislators and District Council members were active participants in its activities. ISCUS, therefore, seems to be a platform in which the CPI acts in collaboration with other parties with the broad objective of popularizing the significance of the concept of Indo-Soviet Friendship. We should, however, take note of the fact that ISCUS is not a class organization of the CPI, but only a front linking the CPI to progressive elements of other classes.

All-India Peace and Solidarity Organization and Indo-German Democratic Republic Friendship

Association are the two other organizations which have their units in Meghalaya and in which the CPI participates along with other political parties. All-India Peace and Solidarity Organization which fights against nuclear war for the promotion of world peace was formed in Meghalaya in 1976. Late Reverend B. M. Pugh was the State Committee President of AIPSO who visited USSR to attend Afro-Asian Solidarity Conference at Baku. From Meghalaya, O. L. Nongtdu, Santosh Das, B. B. Dutta, M. Chakravarty and Robin Rema attended the World Peace Congress held at Prague. D. D. Lapang and D. Dympep were President and General Secretary respectively of Indo-German Democratic Republic Friendship Association.[75]

The Communists' efforts to establish a mass organization for women met with success when in June, 1954, a National Federation of Indian Women was organized at a National Congress of Women held in Calcutta. Because non-Communist participation was desired, the Communists were careful to keep the political content of the meeting at a moderate level. The Congress elected a twenty-nine member Executive Committee with Puspamoyee Bose as President and Anasuya Gyan Chand and Hajrah Begum as Joint Secretaries. Hajrah Begum and a number of other women have been leaders in Communist and Communist-sponsored organizations.[76] The second conference of NFIW took place in Vijayawada in June, 1957, with 353 delegates attending from different States. There were also fraternal delegates from Great Britain, USSR, Rumania and Czechoslovakia. Most resolutions dealt with economic and social questions affecting women, but a demand was also made for the cessation of nuclear weapons testing.[77]

National Federation of Indian Women is one of the various mass organizations of the CPI which have their units in Meghalaya. Meghalaya State Council of NFIW was formed in 1973. Miss Percylina Marak, APHLC MLA, presided over the first conference of NFlW in which delegates from all parts of Meghalaya attended. E. S. Lyngwa and Devika Saikia were President and General Secretary respectively of NFIW. An all-India Conference of NFIW was attended by 25 delegates from Meghalaya. It is significant to observe that in the Meghalaya State Conference of NFIW, more than 85% of the delegates were tribals. Under the NFIW leadership, various women's days were observed in Meghalaya. It is also claimed that the Meghalaya Unit of NFIW conducted eleven schools for the eradication of adult women illiteracy in Meghalaya. At present, however, the organization is not so active as it was in the past.[78] The schools established by it also do not seem to exist.

The story of the Communist dominated mass organizations in India in recent years appears to be one of decline. As Overstreet and Windmiller rightly point out, during World War II, the Communists had almost no competition in the major mass organizations, for the Congress leadership was in jail and the Socialists were underground. When competition began to develop around 1947, the task became more difficult. To this was added the disastrous extremist line pursued by B. T. Ranadive. There has been a growing realization in the CPI that it is extremism or "sectarianism" that has weakened the mass organizations. This has been most evident in the AIKS where too close an adherence to Communist Party policy has meant the loss, from time to time, of important peasant leaders. It is also evident in the student movement, and to a lesser degree in the trade unions.[79] The report of Ajoy Ghosh on the decisions of the Central Committee in May 1954, may be noted in this connection :

> *"Mass organizations, the Central Committee stressed, have to be built and run as real non-party united organizations, organizations which the masses consider to be their own and in whose functioning they have live interest. Such is very often not the case today, not merely in relation to organizations, which are led by reformists, but also in relation to organizations led by Communists. Sectarian methods of running these organizations harm both the Party and the organizations and weaken the movement of the masses".*[80]

But though the mass organizations appear to be weak when viewed from a national perspective, they are undoubtedly strong in certain areas. For example, West Bengal is one State in which the AITUC, the AIKS, the AISF and the NFIW are all strong. As far as Meghalaya is concerned, it seems that none of the mass organizations of the CPI has been able to achieve significant breakthrough in mobilizing different sections of the masses. The trade union movement, in particular, has suffered major setbacks and a number of trade unions formerly affiliated to the AITUC have switched over to the INTUC. NFIW, the women's front, had initially procured the services of some prominent women leaders of Meghalaya who worked for the emancipation of women. But this organization too, has ceased to be active. It may be observed, however, that Indo-Soviet Cultural Society which has earned more credibility and public attention in Meghalaya is not a class organization of the CPI, but a front in which a number of political parties other than the CPI is actively involved. It appears that most mass organizations of the CPI in Meghalaya exist in paper only. In the absence of rapid industrialization, the proletariat has not grown in Meghalaya and hence the mass organizations are instead led by non-tribals essentially belonging to the middle class. Remnants of the tribal mode of production can still be traced in different parts of Meghalaya and sharp class divisions have not emerged as a result of which the Communist ideology has remained more or less irrelevant in the Meghalayan situation. Finally, the growth of an educated elite group in Meghalaya[81] whose aspirations cannot be fulfilled in the Communist scheme of things has further hindered the effective functioning of different mass organizations of the CPI.

References

1. Overstreet and Windmiller, *Communism in India* (Berkeley, 1959), p. 366.
2. Joseph Stalin, *Foundations of Leninism* (New York, 1939), p. 115.
3. Overstreet and Windmiller, *op.cit,* p. 367.
4. *Ibid.,* p. 406.
5. Prabodh Chandra, *Student Movement in India,* (Lahore; AISF, 1938), pp. 53-54.
6. *Ibid.,* pp. 54-55.
7. Overstreet and Windmiller, *op.cit.,* p. 396.
8. *Ibid.,* p. 398.
9. *Loc.cit.*
10. See Prafulla Misra, "Communist Movement in Assam", *North Eastern Affairs,* July-September, 1972, pp. 36-37.
11. *Ibid.,* p. 37.
12. For details, see A. Guha, *Planter Raj to Swaraj, Freedom Struggle and Electoral Politics in Assam 1826-1947* (New Delhi: 1977), p. 323. Also see S.K. Chaube, *Hill Politics in North-East India* (Calcutta, 1973), pp. 73 and 141 and P. Misra, *op.cit.,* p. 37.
13. Information gathered by the author from Umapada Deb.

14. *Ibid.*
15. Author's discussions with Ranjit Kar on 26th March, 1988.
16. *Ibid.*
17. "Public Meeting Against War", a leaflet published by M. Chakravarty in 1984.
18. Relevant leaflets and the certificate obtained from Ranjit Kar and Prafulla Misra.
19. Author's discussions with Ranjit Kar.
20. *Ibid.*
21. *Loc. cit.*
22. Information obtained from Umapada Deb, *op.cit.*
23. Prafulla Misra, "Communist Movement in Assam", *op.cit.*, p. 38.
24. Information obtained from Umapada Deb, *op.cit.*
25. Author's discussions with Ranjit Kar.
26. Overstreet and Windmiller, *op.cit.*, pp. 367-368.
27. S. D. Punekar, *Trade Unionism in India* (Bombay, 1948), p. 91.
28. *Meerut Sessions Judgment,* p. 61.
29. Overstreet and Windmiller, *op.cit.*, p. 369.
30. *Meerut Sessions Judgment*, *op.cit.*, p. 179.
31. See M. N. Roy, "The Indian Trade Union Congress", *Inprecor*, VI, (Feb. 18, 1926), p. 191.
32. Mitra, (ed), *Indian Annual Register,* 1928, II, 503-504.
33. *Meerut Sessions Judgment, op.cit.*, p. 227.
34. Overstreet and Windmiller, *op.cit.*, p. 373.

35. *Ibid.*, pp. 373-374.
36. *Ibid.*, pp. 374-375.
37. As no published documents on the AITUC in Meghalaya is available, this account had to be based on the author's discussions with veteran trade union leader of North East India, Binoy Lahiri, on the 3rd of April, 1988, in Shillong.
38. *Ibid.*
39. *Ibid.*
40. *Ibid.*
41. *Ibid.*
42. *Ibid.*
43. *Ibid.*
44. *Ibid.*
45. *The Shillong Times,* September 17, 2005, p. 3.
46. Overstreet and Windmiller, *op. cit.,* p. 384.
47. N. G. Ranga, *Revolutionary Peasants* (New Delhi, 1949), p. 60.
48. Overstreet and Windmiller, *op. cit.,* p. 384.
49. Ranga, *op. cit.,* p. 69.
50. Overstreet and Windmiller, *op. cit.,* p. 385.
51. See E. M. S. Nambodiripad, *The Peasant in National Economic Reconstruction* (Delhi, 1954), p. 92.
52. Overstreet and Windmiller, *op.cit.,* pp. 392-395.
53. Because of the non-availability of published documents, the account on Kisan Sabha has been based on the author's discussions with Binoy Lahiri, dated the 3rd April, 1988, in Shillong.
54. *Ibid.*

55. *Ibid.*
56. Benoy Lahiri, "Land and Land Relations in Meghalaya", a paper presented during a Symposium on "Tribal Demography and Development"(with special reference to North East India), May 27-29, 1985, at Mayurbhanj Seminar Hall, NEHU.
57. For a detailed account on the CPI's programme for agriculture, see *Draft Programme of the Meghalaya Coordination Committee of the CPI,* 1973, pp. 11-12.
58. Discussions with Lahiri, *op.cit.*
59. The term "fellow traveller" is broadly defined by Overstreet and Windmiller as those who accept Communist ideology, support a large measure of Party policy, or frequently join known Party members in common political activity. They, however, call for utmost caution in the use of the term. See Overstreet and Windmiller, *op.cit.,* pp. 440-441.
60. *ISCUS,* II (Spring, 1955), p. 84.
61. *Crossroads,* III (March 21, 1952), pp. 8-9.
62. *ISCUS,* I, (July, 1954), p. 3.
63. *Ibid.,* I (January, 1954), back cover.
64. *Ibid.,* Ill (Winter, 1956), pp. 1, 69.
65. Author's discussions with M. Chakravorty in Shillong on 1st May, 1988.
66. Author's discussions with Prafulla Misra in Shillong on 26th March, 1988. The information obtained from Misra was later compared with that obtained from Chakravarty for authenticity.

67. *Ibid.*
68. Author's discussions with M. Chakravarty, *op. cit.*
69. *Ibid.*
70. Author's discussions with P. Misra, *op. cit.*
71. Author's discussions with Chakravarty, *op. cit.*
72. Author's discussions with Misra, *op. cit.*
73. Author's discussions with Chakravarty, *op. cit.*
74. Overstreet and Windmiller, *op. cit.,* p. 411.
75. Author's discussions with P. Misra in Shillong, dated the 26th March, 1988.
76. Overstreet and Windmiller, *op. cit.,* pp. 402-403.
77. *New Age* (Weekly), IV (June 23, 1957), p. 16.
78. Author's discussions with P. Misra on 25th March, 1988, in Shillong.
79. Overstreet and Windmiller, *op. cit.,* p. 404.
80. Ajoy Ghosh, "On the Decisions of the Central Committee", *New Age* (Weekly), I (May 2, 1954), p. 4.
81. See articles by B. P. Misra, P. N. Dutta, B. B. Dutta and S. K. Chaube in B. Datta Ray (ed.), *The Emergence and Role of Middle Class in North-East India* (New Delhi, 1983).

4

Meghalaya CPI and State Assembly Elections - An Assessment

We have seen how the CPI's front organizations work to mobilize people at the grass-roots level. Let us now try to analyse the CPI's performance in the first three Assembly Elections in Meghalaya in order to assess its impact on the political life of the State.

The CPI has contested all the three Elections to the Meghalaya Legislative Assemby that were held in 1972, 1978 and 1983 respectively. Some of the prominent members of the CPI have frankly admitted that the party's main consideration in contesting all these elections was to utilize the opportunity for propagating and popularizing the CPI's views and the ideals it stands for. Indeed the CPI did not, at the time of these elections, seriously expect to win any seats in the State Legislative Assembly.[1]

The 1972 Election Manifesto of Meghalaya Coordination Committee of the CPI stressed the need for harnessing all the resources of the new-born State of Meghalaya for a rapid advance towards a prosperous future. The CPI brought to the notice of the electorate the party's strong support expressed both inside and outside parliament, for elevation of

Meghalaya to a full-fledged State. The party projected itself as the most consistent fighter for rights of the toiling people, the peasants, the workers, the middle class and tribal people of the country. The CPI went on to highlight its campaign against the Imperialist grip over Indian economy and the Imperialist pressure on India's policy and mobilization of public opinion by the party in favour of a closer relationship between India and the Socialist countries headed by Soviet Union.[2]

The Meghalaya Co-ordination Committee, Communist Party of India, placed the broad outline of a programme for a rapid advance of Meghalaya towards a prosperous future which included programmes on agriculture, industries, transport and communication, public health, education and for workers and employees, minorities and for Shillong in particular.[3]

The party's candidates in the 1972 Assembly Election were :

Binoy Lahiri - Malki (U K and J Hills)

Rosendra Hajong - Selsella (Garo Hills)

It appears from a close look at the CPI's Election Manifesto of 1972 that the party's programme for Meghalaya was a response to the needs and aspirations of all sections of the lower strata of the Society - peasants, industrial workers, minorities - both tribal and non-tribal and the poor in general. The CPI programme seemed to bring under its purview almost all aspects of the life of these different sections of people - health, education, working conditions, civic facilities and protection of cultural, linguistic, religious and political rights of minorities.[4]

In the General Elections to the Meghalaya Legislative Assembly held in March 1972, the district-wise position of the CPI was as follows :

Table 1. General Elections: Meghalaya Legislative Assembly March 1972

Sl.No.	*District*	*Total valid votes polled*	*Number and percentage of valid votes polled by CPI*
1.	Khasi Hills	118,098	715 (0.6%)
2.	Garo Hills	49,753	467 (0.9%)
	Total	167,851	1,182 (0.71% approximately)

Source: Meghalaya Election Handbook, February 1983, p. 45.

Table 2. Number and Percentage of Valid Votes Polled by CPI vis-a-vis Total Electorate in 1972

Sl.No.	*District*	*Total electorate*	*Valid votes polled by CPI and percentage thereof*
1.	Khasi Hills	2,15,168	715 (0.33%)
2.	Garo Hills	1,48,286	467 (0.31%)
	Total	3,63,454	1,182 (0.32% approximately)

Source: Meghalaya Election Handbook, March 1972, p. 11.

The CPI lost both seats it contested in the 1972 Election. The party's candidate from Selsella Constituency in Garo Hills also forfeited his security deposit.[5] In Malki Constituency, Binoy Lahiri of CPI lost to Upstar Kharbuli, an Independent candidate, by a margin of 1,631 votes. Interestingly, the CPI candidate was the nearest rival of the elected candidate.[6] In Selsella Constituency, William Cecil R. Marak of Congress defeated Rosendra Hajong of CPI, the margin of victory being 2,083 votes. Again, the CPI candidate was the winner's nearest rival.[7] It may be noted that in the elections of March 1972, the CPI bagged the maximum number of its votes in the Khasi Hills. However, the party's position in the electoral map of Meghalaya as a whole was insignificant and as such, the CPI was in no position to make any impact on the politics of the newborn State. It appears as though the radical programme presented by the CPI was not sufficient to impress the voters.

The general election to the Meghalaya Legislative Assembly, February 1978, was held at a crucial period of Indian history. The three decades of Congress rule at the Centre had come to an end and the Janata Party came to power with the slogan of fighting against the Emergency misdeeds of the Congress regime and of restoring democracy. The CPI identified the Janata Party as a conglomeration of various forces in which there was a domination of Rightists and Communal forces. The CPI also felt that the masses of Indians who expected some change in their living condition under the Janata Raj were soon getting disillusioned. The party further pointed out that because of a split in the Congress, its capacity to function even as a viable opposition had been in doubt. The dire state of the Congress and the lack of political cohesion within the Janata Party had, according to the CPI, given rise to a sort of political instability, which demanded more than ever before, unity of the Left and Democratic forces for providing a real alternative to the country. The CPI mentioned in this connection its own consistent efforts to bring about the unity of Left and Democratic forces, including even those in the regional parties.[9]

The CPI clarified that its participation in the State Assembly election of 1978 was motivated by the need to rouse the people of Meghalaya to the necessity of a strong unity of all the Left and Democratic forces, which could guarantee the defence of the country's sovereignty, the protection of the rights of the toiling people including the Harijans, Tribals and other weaker sections and defence of the nationally accepted basic policies of the country.[10]

In its Election Manifesto, the CPI also claimed to have fought against rising prices; it conducted campaigns for industrial development in the public sector, to create jobs for the youth; the party campaigned for cadestral survey of land and preparation of records of rights so that the peasants might secure cheap credit from the nationalized Banks and would not remain at the mercy of money-lenders only. The CPI demanded extension of medical facilities in the rural areas, supply of drinking water to the rural people, extension of the public distribution system in order to give relief to the people from the ever-soaring prices of essential commodities.[11]

The CPI found no contradiction between the legitimate rights of the tribal majority and the non-tribal minorities who were permanent inhabitants of the State. At the same time, the party stood firmly for defending the constitutional safeguards provided for the tribal people. The party believed that united efforts of the working people, both the majority and the minority, alone could guarantee the rights and privileges of both. The CPI felt that it was the economic development of the State which could solve the problems of both the majority and the minority.[12]

The CPI Election Manifesto drew the voters' attention to the party's fight against eviction of peasants and against attempts for demolition of way-side shops. The CPI felt that its fight for modernization of agriculture, for emancipation of peasants, for industrialization and for an all-round development of the State could be further strengthened if the party had some representatives inside the State Legislature where policies are formulated.[13] The Meghalaya State Council of the CPI nominated the following candidates for the constituencies mentioned against their names:

Khasi Hills

1. Binoy Lahiri for Pynthorumkhrah
2. Dalington Dympep for Umroi
3. Jokendra Lanong for Jaiaw.

Garo Hills

1. Robin Rema for Dalu.

In the 1978 Assembly Election, the CPI's position in the districts in which it contested was as given below.

Table 3. General Elections: Meghalaya Legislative Assembly, February 1978

Sl.No.	*District*	*Total valid votes polled*	*Number and percentage of valid votes polled by CPI*
1.	East Khasi Hills	1,33,433	1,851 (1.38%)
	(a) Shillong Sub-division	1,09,280	1,750 (1.62%)
	(b) Ri Bhoi Sub-division	24,153	101 (0.42%)
2.	West Garo Hills	97,558	510 (0.52%)
	(a) Tura Sub-division	88,019	510 (0.58%)
	Total	2,42,713	2,361 (0.97% approximately)

Source: Meghalaya Election Handbook, February, 1983, p. 44. As only those Subdivisions from which the CPI contested have been included in this table, the percentage of votes polled by the CPI had to be worked out by the author herself.

Table 4. Number and Percentage of valid votes polled by CPI vis-a-vis Total Electorate in 1978

Sl.No.	*District*	*Total electorate*	*Valid votes polled by CPI and percentage of electorate*
1.	East Khasi Hills	2,01,700	1,851 (0.92%)
	(a) Shillong Sub-division	1,62,058	1,750 (1.08%)
	(b) Ri Bhoi Sub-division	39,642	101 (0.25%)
2.	West Garo Hills	1,56,278	510 (0.33%)
	(a) Tura Sub-division	1,38,974	510 (0.37%)
	Total	5,85,023	2,361 (0.43% approxi-mately)

Source: Meghalaya Election Handbook, February 1983, p. 48.

As in the Assembly Elections of 1972, the CPI failed to open its account in the 1978 General Election also. From Pynthorumkhrah, Binoy Lahiri secured 786 votes. Dalington Dympep secured 101 votes from Umroi, Jokendro Lanong captured 964 votes from Jaiaw and from Dalu, Robin Rema secured 510 votes. All the CPI nominees forfeited their security deposits. Although the CPI's performance showed some improvement over its position in the previous election (percentage of votes increasing by .206%), this cannot be regarded as significant because there was an increase in the number of candidates set up by the CPI. Thus, the CPI still had a long way to go before it could emerge as a viable political force in Meghalaya's electoral arena.

We now pass on to the Assembly Election of 1983. In its Election Manifesto for the 1983 General Election, the CPI drew the electorate's attention to the accentuation of the crisis of the capitalist path pursued by the bourgeois class in India.[14] The party systematically presented a list of retrograde economic policies pursued by the Janata regime and the Congress Government (during the emergency and for the two years after returning to power in 1980) in the form of more and more concessions to the monopolists, transnational corporations etc., of allowing the private sector to penetrate and capture strategic fields reserved till then for Public Sector, of massive borrowings from international financial institutions on terms that undermined national self-reliance, of shifting more and more burdens on the working people instead of mobilizing resources for development from the profiteering classes and so on.[15] Having thus criticized the bourgeoisie policy at the all India level, the CPI stated that people's expectations about the regeneration of the stagnant economy of Meghalaya were not fulfilled by successive governments that came to power during the last ten years. The peasants were not paid remunerative prices for their products. CPI demanded industrialization on the basis of raw materials available in the State and to impart technical training to the youths of Meghalaya to be able to man the industries. It asserted that as a result of the growth of private proprietorship on communal land, there had been concentration of land in fewer hands and growing pauperization of the actual cultivators many of whom were becoming sharecroppers and agricultural labourers. There was no statutory recognition of sharecropping and therefore, there was no legally recognized uniform pattern of sharing the crops between the landlord and their sharecroppers. Though minimum wage was fixed for the agricultural labourers, the CPI found in despair that there was no machinery to enforce it. The party felt that very little was done by the successive State Governments to protect the peasantry and pointed out the hollowness of all the talks about "protection of the tribal interest".[16]

The Meghalaya State Council of CPI reiterated its faith on the programme it chalked out in the 1978 Election Manifesto for all-round prosperity of Meghalaya. As part of this programme, the CPI claimed to have organized the workers and employees in their respective trade unions and helped them in their struggle for wage increase, preserving Trade Union rights etc. The CPI claimed that its fight for fixation of minimum wages for different categories of workers succeeded in most cases in getting the same implemented. The party also claimed to have organized peasants in the rural areas and fought to protect their interests as well. While the CPI found no contradiction between the legitimate rights of the tribal majority and permanent inhabitants of Meghalaya among the non-tribal minorities, the party firmly stood for defending the constitutional safeguards provided for the tribal people. The CPI maintained that its fight for modernization of agriculture and emancipation of peasants, for industrialization of the State in the public sector and its demand for the State takeover of primary education and free education for all upto Class X and for all-round development of the State could receive a boost if the party had some representation within the State Legislature.[17] The CPI's candidates in the 1983 General Election were:

Khasi Hills	Dalington Dympep	-Mawkhar
	Jokendro Lanong	-Mawprem
	Binoy Lahiri	-Laban
Jaintia Hills	Babyson Pakyntein	-War Jaintia
Garo Hills	Bharat Sangma	-Baghmara

Robin Rema -Tura

Nripendralal Mishra -Dalu

In the General Elections to the Meghalaya Legislative Assembly, February 1983, the CPI's position in the different districts of Meghalaya was as follows:

Table 5. General Elections: Meghalaya Legislative Assembly, February 1983

Sl.No.	*District*	*Total valid votes polled*	*Number and percentage of valid votes polled by CPI*
1.	Jaintia Hills	71,448	194 (0.27%)
2.	East Khasi Hills	1,74,548	1,212 (0.69%)
	(a) Shillong	28,779	1,212 (0.83%)
3.	West Garo Hills	1,28,397	1,036 (0.80%)
	(a) Baghmara Sub-division	12,828	297 (2.31%)
	(b) Tura	1,15,569	739 (0.63%)
	Total	3,74,393	2,442 (0.65% approxi-mately)

Source: Meghalaya Election Handbook, February, 1983, p. 42.

Table 6. Number and Percentage of valid votes polled by CPI vis-a-vis Total Electorate

Sl.No.	*District*	*Total electorate*	*Valid votes polled by CPI and percentage of electorate*
1.	Jaintia Hills	96,474	194 (0.20%)
2.	East Khasi Hills	2,54,906	1,212 (0.48%)
	(a) Shillong	2,09,885	1,212 (0.57%)
3.	West Garo Hills	1,77,189	1,036 (0.58%)
	(a) Baghmara Sub-division	18,949	297 (1.57%)
	(b) Tura	1,58,240	739 (0.46%)
	Total	5,28,569	2,442 (0.46%) approxi- mately)

Source: Meghalaya Election Handbook, February, 1983, p. 46.

Thus, in the 1983 Assembly Election, the CPI's dismal performance continued with the defeat of all of its nominated candidates. The candidates had to bear with the additional humiliation of their security deposits being forfeited. For the first time, the CPI fielded a candidate in Jaintia Hills from War Jaintia Constituency. But its nominee, Mr. Babyson Pakyntein could capture 194 votes (0.27% of total valid votes polled) only. He lost to an Independent candidate by a huge margin of 3,205 votes. From Mawkhar Constituency, Mr. Dalington Dympep polled a total of 97 valid votes and was defeated by the APHLC candidate by a margin of 1,675 votes. In Mawprem Constituency, Mr. Jokendro Lanong secured 527 votes and lost to the Indian National Congress candidate by 2,848 votes. From Laban Assembly Constituency, the Indian National Congress candidate defeated Shri Binoy Lahiri of CPI by 2,000 votes. The CPI nominee captured 588 votes only. In Baghmara Constituency, Mr. Bharat Sangma of CPI secured 297 votes and was defeated by Capt. Williamson A. Sangma by a large margin of 4,673 votes. In the prestigious Tura Assembly Constituency, Mr. Robin Rema of CPI lost to the Indian National Congress candidate, the margin of defeat being 3,421 votes. The CPI nominee had secured only 333 votes out of 10,016 valid votes polled. From Dalu, Shri Nripendralal Misra of CPI polled 406 votes and was defeated by the Indian National Congress candidate by a margin of 1,455 votes.[18]

After discussing the CPI's performance in the three Assembly Elections of Meghalaya in general, we shall now proceed to examine the probable impact which the CPI's election manifestoes might have had on the voters of different constituencies. It is interesting to note that it was part of the CPI's election strategy to shift from one constituency to another in each election. In 1972, the CPI chose to contest from Malki and Selsella Constituencies. In 1978, the party opted for Pynthorumkhrah, Umroi, Jaiaw and Dalu constituencies respectively. In 1983, again, the CPI's contesting arena shifted to Mawkhar, Mawprem, Laban, War Jaintia, Baghmara, Tura and Dalu constituencies. Thus, the CPI contested from Dalu twice, whereas a number of other constituencies were taken up by turn as if on an experimental basis, to judge the mood and sentiments of voters. This also shows that the CPI did not work consistently in the constituencies to win the voters. Instead of sticking to particular constituencies, the CPI promptly shifted to other constituencies after losing in those constituencies.

In the 1972 Assembly Election in Meghalaya, Binoy Lahiri of CPI contested from Malki, a constituency which at that time covered areas like Police Bazar, Pynthorumkhrah, Oakland, Jail Road, Dhankheti and extended upto the Tripura Castle area. Tribal voters constituted the majority of the electorate in Malki.[19]

As the CPI nominee, Lahiri feels that his party's prospects of winning from Malki could have brightened had there been a straight contest between the three major parties - CPI, Congress and APHLC. However, Congress and APHLC did not set up any official candidate and sponsored some independent candidates. In Oakland, European Ward and Forest Colony, there were several Assamese voters. The APHLC, therefore, set up an Assamese candidate as independent in order to divide the Assamese votes.[20] Now, Malki being an urban constituency, the CPI's detailed programme on agriculture might not have impressed the voters. However, the party's promise for creation of wide job opportunities by rapid industrialization and provision of various civic facilities for Shillong could have had some appeal to the electorate. Besides, the CPI's assurance for safeguarding the rights and interests of minorities could have fetched it some minority votes. But, as we have seen, only 0.6% of total valid votes were polled in favour of the CPI nominee. The lofty promises made by the party seemed to have made little impact on the Malki voters, because the promises did not appear likely to be translated into political action.

In 1972, the CPI also chose to contest from the Selsella constituency of Garo Hills. Gandopara, Dabakgiri, Selsella, Agipeng, Garobadha, Harigao, Chamaguri, Rochonpara etc. were some of the areas falling under the Selsella Constituency. Although most of the voters in Selsella are agriculturists, Selsella may be regarded as a developed rural area, it being the Block Development Headquarters. Garos are in a majority in Selsella, with small tribes like Hajongs, Koches and a few Mans also forming part of the electorate. In Garobadha, some Bengalis and Biharis, too, are enrolled as voters. Now, in Selsella, the CPI is popular among the Hajongs, plains cultivators and non-tribals.[21] Thus, the CPI member himself admits that the party is unpopular among other communities. Here, the CPI's programme on agriculture should have served the needs of the voters. The party's proposal for self-employment in cottage industries, demand for provision of medical facilities, establishment of more primary schools etc. could also have served to satisfy the aspirations of the electorate. Rosendra Hajong being the CPI nominee from Selsella, the CPI could have counted on some Hajong votes also. However, as Robin Rema, a prominent Communist leader from Garo Hills, admits, the political scenario in 1972 was not favourable for the CPI to win from Selsella. Meghalaya was just born and the regional parties were more popular.[22] The CPI's ambiguous role in the hill state movement could have had some adverse impact on its image in Meghalaya.

In the General Election of 1972 in Meghalaya, none of the regional parties had any programme of movement on mass issues before the people, neither did they project any socio-economic programme during the election and always harped on the slogan of 'protection of the tribal identity and protection of the tribal customs and traditions' and the slogan against the influx of foreigners. The CPI, on the contrary, projected an economic programme and sought to support democratic political rights and had some mass movements on different issues, but its influence was too weak to have any considerable impact on the political life of the State or on electoral politics.[23] As P. C. Biswas observes, electoral politics in Meghalaya mainly centred round some generalizations and was influenced by personalities rather than any political or economic programme. The people were left politically very backward and they did not go through any sort of mass movement or general popular issues like increase of prices, exploitation of local producers by the wholesale businessmen or any democratic issues and they could not demarcate the respective roles of different regional and the All India parties from one another through their own experiences. The ordinary people did not and do not get any opportunity to judge which party actually stood for what and how their class interests could be best protected or achieved by supporting which party. Whatever mass or class organization of the peasants and the workers existed in Meghalaya, exerted very little influence on electoral politics as such.[24]

In the 1978 Assembly Election, the CPI fielded Binoy Lahiri for Pynthorumkhrah - a constituency formed after delimitation of Laitumkhrah, Malki and Mawlai constituencies. Pynthorumkhrah now included Pynthorbah, Nongkhardot, Rynjah, Forest Colony, Jail Road, Oakland, Nongmynsong etc.[25] Here, the non-tribal voters had a slight majority over the tribal voters. Now, in 1978, the CPI like all other non-Congress parties tried to capitalize on the anti-Congress wave generated in the country by the emergency excesses. The party also pointed out the basic weaknesses of the Janata Alliance and stressed the need for a strong unity of all the Left and Democratic forces. The CPI drew the voters' attention to price rise and the alarming growth of unemployment and the party's fight against both of these problems. The CPI also sought to safeguard the legitimate rights of the non-tribal minorities along with those of the tribal majority. The CPI manifesto thus appeared to provide something for various sections of the population in an urban constituency. In the 1978 contest, a number of tribal and non-tribal candidates took the field. In Pynthorumkhrah also, the CPI candidate could have drawn a large number of votes in case of a straight contest. But supporters of the leftist parties were divided by the setting up of a CPI (M) and a Naxalite candidate as independents both of whom were sponsored by the Congress. CPI leaders claim that the Naxalite candidate being a Brahmin, casteism also played a significant role in Jail Road and Pynthorumkhrah areas. All these factors culminated to influence the outcome of the contest and finally the Congress emerged victorious as a result of the division of votes on various lines.[26] Indeed, the leftist candidates among them bagged 2,111 votes as against 1,575 votes captured by the elected Congress candidate.[27]

Dalington Dympep was the CPI nominee for Umroi in the 1978 Election. Umroi Constituency included Kyrdem Kulai, Lum Nongrim, Nonglum,

Pynthor, Mawbri, Mawshut, Mawtneng, Lumshyiap, Mawkduk, Sumer, Umroi, Bhoirymbong, Mawlyndep, Nongsder, Klew, Umbir etc.[28] In this rural constituency, tribals constituted the majority of the electorate, although there was a sizable number of non-tribal voters as well who were employed in Meghalaya State Electricity Board (MSEB). Now, the CPI's demand for protection of the legitimate rights of the non-tribal minorities and its fight against unemployment and rising prices were meant for the consumption of different sections of employees. The party's campaign for welfare of the peasantry could have appealed to the rural, tribal voters. But, as Mr. Dympep himself points out, the CPI did not have a strong support base in Umroi. Moreover, he claims that the poll verdict was to a large extent influenced by money power in the sense that voters could be easily misled and corrupted by money, due to lack of political consciousness. Village headmen and other leaders who command a lot of respect and authority among the rural masses could be influenced by money for forcing the voters to vote for the candidate backed by a particular party. He further claims that anti-Communist propaganda engineered by the Church ruined the possibilities of any electoral dividends the CPI might have hoped to reap in Umroi.[29] The CPI was also severely handicapped by lack of adequate funds which restrained it from spending lavishly on campaigning etc. Thus, the party's chances of winning from Umroi were rather remote. It is, however, difficult to verify the views expressed by the CPI nominee.

Jokendro Lanong of CPI contested from the Jaiaw Constituency in the 1978 election. Apart from Jaiaw proper, this constituency also included Garikhana, Qualapatty, Lower Mawprem etc.[30] Whereas voters in Jaiaw are mostly tribals, in Garikhana and Lower Mawprem, several non-tribals are enrolled as part of the electorate.[31] Given the nature of the electorate, it appears that the Communist Party's policies and objectives were unlikely to suit the interests of the majority of the voters. The CPI's attempt to equalize the interests of the non-tribal minorities with those of the tribal majority might have hurt the sentiments of the tribal voters. The non-tribals, on the other hand, might have felt that the Congress or even the regional parties were in a better position than the CPI to safeguard their interests. The political climate and voters' sentiments being thus unfavourable, the CPI could not put up an impressive electoral performance in Jaiaw.

Robin Rema was the CPI nominee from Dalu Constituency of Garo Hills in 1978. Dalu included Nokchi, Tarapara, Dalu, Kujikora, Gangbanga, Ramchengga, Dalugao, Kapasipara, Sibbari, Gasuapara, Thopaskura etc.[32] Dalu had an electorate of over 10,000 out of which more than 4,000 were Garos, more than 1,300 Koches, more than 1,200 Hajongs, about 2,000 non-tribals comprising Biharis and Bengalis and about 3,000

Dalus. Dalu may be regarded as a developed rural area which is a business center as also the Block Headquarter.[33] CPI's campaigns for cadestral survey of land and preparation of records of rights as also for extension of medical facilities in the rural area, for supplying drinking water to the rural people, for extension of the public distribution system in order to give relief to the people from the ever-soaring prices of essential commodities etc.[34] could have impressed the voters of Dalu. Now, in Dalu, the CPI was popular among Hajongs, some non-tribals and Koches. There were also some CPI sympathizers among local Garos, but they were not prepared to cast their votes in favour of the CPI nominee because of anti-Communist propaganda by the Church among local Garos, who were mostly Christians.[35]

It may be noted that during the 1978 General Election, as a part of the main plank of 'protection of tribal identity' - a demand for 'quit outsiders' was accepted as the main slogan of all the parties (regional) and the Congress was attacked as the 'Outsider's Party' and not willing or capable of preserving tribal identity of the State.[36] The CPI's stand on this particular issue was rather vague. As stated above, while the party stood for defending the constitutional safeguards provided for the tribal people, the party found no contradiction between the legitimate rights of the tribal majority and the non-tribal minorities who were permanent inhabitants of the State. This position adopted by the CPI might have bred suspicion in the minds of the majority of tribal voters who played safe by turning to the regional parties as the true protectors of their interests.

In the 1983 General Election to the Meghalaya Legislative Assembly, the CPI fielded Dalington Dympep as its candidate for Mawkhar constituency. Mawkhar constituency included Mawkhar proper, Umsohsun, Wahingdoh, Riatsamthiah, Mission Compound, Wahthapbru, Bara Bazar, Police Bazar and the Sweepers' Colony. Now, Mawkhar proper, Umsohsun, Wahingdoh, Riatsamthiah and Mission Compound are predominantly inhabited by Khasis who belong either to the indigenous religion or are Christians. The residents of the Sweepers' Colony belong to the Sikh religion and the Marwaris and other minority groups (like Sindhis, Nepalese, Bengalees, Assamese, Biharis etc.) around the Barabazar and Police Bazar areas belong to the Hindu religion.[37] The Congress (I) and the Regional or State Parties, besides citing their achievements in maintaining the distinct identity of the tribal people and solving the local problems of the people to a certain extent, laid stress on two important issues - education and foreign nationals' issue.

The APHLC, e.g., claimed that it would detect and deport the foreign nationals who had unlawfully entered into the State. The CPI, however, did not mention any clear cut measures in this direction. In a very subtle way, it mentioned that there was no contradiction between the legitimate rights of the tribal majority and the non-tribal minorities who were the permanent inhabitants of the state. A peculiar fact observed by Bawri in the Mawkhar constituency was that a non-tribal would cast his vote for a tribal candidate and enjoy his confidence than give it to a non-tribal who would serve his own interest. Taking advantage of this, the tribal candidates employed all the election techniques to capture as many non-tribal votes as possible.[38] Now, although the CPI fielded a tribal candidate for Mawkhar constituency, the resources at the party's disposal could in no way match those of other prominent parties. In an interview with some of the voters, Bawri found that they received money or intoxicating drinks from the candidates in return of their promise to vote for them.[39] According to Mr. Dympep, the religious factor also played a crucial role in influencing the opinion of the voters in Mawkhar. While leaflets carrying anti-Communist propaganda were distributed among the Christians, films were also shown depicting how Christians were being persecuted by Communists.[40] The CPI's ambiguous stand on the Foreigners' issue, its lack of resources and above all, the religious factor - all these were responsible for the CPI's setback in the Mawkhar election.

In 1983, Jokendra Lanong of CPI contested from Mawprem constituency which covered Barapathar, Upper Mawprem, Naspati Ghari, Lady Keane,

Kench's Trace, Rilbong, Jhalupara etc.[41] The electorate was composed mostly of Nepalis and Bengalis, while a large number of Biharis and a few Jaintias - were also enrolled as voters.[42] Now, in Mawprem, the Congress was the most dominant party. Dhruba Nath Joshi, its nominee, had won from Mawprem in the 1978 Assembly Election and had a fairly secure support base among the non-tribals - particularly among the Nepalis and Bengalis. In 1983, the main contest was between D. N. Joshi and H. S. Sawian, an independent candidate. The CPI's position in Mawprem was far too weak to make any significant impact on the electoral scene. The votes were more or less evenly divided between Joshi and Sawian and the CPI nominee came out with a poor third position and also had his security deposit forfeited. It seems that the CPI's promise for safeguarding the interests of non-tribal minorities could not fully convince the majority of the voters in Mawprem who were not ready to rely on the CPI for the protection of their rights.

Binoy Lahiri was set up as the CPI nominee for Laban Assembly Constituency in 1983. Lum Kartik, Civil Hospital, Barik, Survey of India, Keating Road, Madan Laban, Lumparing etc.[43] were the localities which fell under the Laban Constituency. Bengalis constituted the majority of the electorate in Laban, although a few Assamese from Bishnupur area and some Khasis were also enrolled as voters.[44] In accordance with an electoral adjustment with the CPI (M) in 1983, the CPI decided to leave one of the three non-tribal dominated constituencies - Laban, Pynthorumkhrah and Mawprem, for the CPI (M). The latter chose to contest from Pynthorumkhah and the remaining two constituencies were reserved for the CPI. Lahiri points out with a great deal of frustration that the CPI fell victim to a well-calculated strategy employed by other parties according to which as many candidates as possible were set up in constituencies in which Communist candidates contested. According to him, this was done in order to ensure that a Communist candidate was never elected to the Assembly. The division of votes that followed as a result of the participation of several candidates had a lot to do with the CPI's defeat in most of the constituencies from which it contested.[45] There might have been a grain of truth in the view expressed by Lahiri, for a look at the list of candidates shows that as many as ten candidates had contested from Laban in 1983. Out of these ten candidates, one each was fielded by Congress, CPI, APHLC (All Party Hill Leaders' Conference), HSPDP (Hill State Peoples' Democratic Party) and Janata, while the remaining five contested as independent candidates. Apart from the Congress nominee who was eventually elected with 2,588 votes to his credit, only the APHLC candidate could secure a respectable number of votes and the rest of the candidates, including the CPI nominee, had their security deposits forfeited. It also appears that the CPI was not viewed as competent enough to protect the rights of the non-tribal minorities.

The CPI fielded Bharat Sangma as its candidate for Baghmara constituency of Garo Hills in the 1983 Election. Baghmara which has now been declared a town is also the Block and Sub-division Headquarter. Apart from Baghmara proper, this constituency includes Mindikgiri, Gittinggiri, Siju-Songmong, Rongsu-Agal, Rewak-Songmong, Halwa-Attong, Kansi, Gurpani-Bibra, Dabit-Bibra, Bhawanipur, Nekora, Nillwagiri, Gaobari, Wagesik, Malikona, Dambuk-Aga, Dallenggittim, Mahadeo, Rongara etc.[46] Garos constitute the majority of the population in Baghmara. Very few Bengalis and Biharis may also be found in the Baghmara Bazar area who migrated from erstwhile East Pakistan after partition. Garos being in a majority among the voters, a candidate had to muster maximum support from this section in order to win from Baghmara. But the CPI was in a disadvantageous position in this regard, as the party was not very popular among the Garo majority.[47] Moreover, the CPI had to confront the Congress veteran, Williamson Sangma, who, over the years, had built up a strong citadel in Baghmara. The CPI, therefore, was in no position to snatch the Baghmara seat in the face of such heavy odds.

As in 1978, the CPI chose to contest from Dalu in 1983 also. Dalu constituency now included Tarapara, Bhoirakupi, Dhopakura, Nokehi, Chandubui, Dalugao, Barengapara, Kujikora, Gangbanga, Jatrakona, Gasuapara, Ramchengga, Kapasipara, Sibbari etc.[48] However, Nripendralal Mishra was given the party ticket in preference to Robin Rema, for being a local resident. The population structure of Dalu in 1983 remained the same as in 1978, because there was no influx. The religious factor which contributed to the CPI's defeat in 1978 similarly had its impact on the voters in 1983 also. As we have noted earlier, the Garos constituted the majority among the voters in Dalu who were mostly Christians.[49] Robin Rema expressed the view that the anti-religious credentials that were thrust upon the communists through propaganda by the Church might have dissuaded the majority of the Garos from voting for the CPI. The question is - whether this opinion is based on facts.

For the first time since the general election of 1972, the CPI set up a candidate for Tura Constituency in 1983. Tura Constituency covered areas like Masumatiagiri, Tura Chandmary, Rongkon, Durakantragiri, Tura Hawakhana, Lower Babupara, Police Compound, Tura Bazar, Fancy Valley, Dobasipara, Daranggiri, Matchakolgiri, Kamipara etc.[50] Robin Rema who contested from Dalu in 1978 was now the CPI nominee for Tura. Now, in an urban constituency like Tura, the electorate was of a mixed nature, including both non-tribals and local Garos, but the former enjoyed a clear majority over the latter. As Robin Rema pointed out, the support of the non-tribal voters was the most important factor for winning any election from Tura. Neither was the Congress (I) organizationally very strong in Tura, nor could it boast of a popular ideology. However, it enjoyed overwhelming support of the non-tribals who relied on the Congress (I) for protection and relief. The trading community, too, turned to the Congress for safeguarding their economic interests, because by virtue of its rule over the centre, the Congress enjoyed the power of patronage. Among the local Garos, of course, the Congress was not very popular. But the Congress (I) more than compensated this lack of popularity by capturing a large chunk of non-tribal votes. As long as the CPI could not earn the confidence of this section of voters, it could not expect to win from Tura.[51]

Babyson Pakyntein was given the CPI nomination for War-Jaintia Assembly Constituency in 1983. War-Jaintia included the areas of Mustein, Mupyut, Jarain, Thangbuli, Amlarem, Mawlong, Padubah, Khonglah, Kudengthymmai, Nongbarehrim, Laminshnong, Sohkha Mission, Darrang, Shnongpdeng, Dawki, Nongtalang, Pdengshakap, Amjalong, Syndai Shnong etc.[52] War-Jaintia had an electorate dominated by Jaintias, although a few non-tribal businessmen were included as voters in Dawki.[53] As Prafulla Misra pointed out in course of a discussion, the Communist Party did not command sufficient influence in War Jaintia. The purpose of joining the electoral battle in War Jaintia was simply to politicize the voters in that constituency. Obviously, there was no possibility of the CPI winning from War Jaintia.[54]

Having examined the electoral performance of the CPI in the Meghalaya Assembly Elections of 1972,

1978 and 1983, we propose to analyse the subsequent elections of 1988, 1993, 1998 and 2003 with the help of the following tables:

Table 7. CPI and State Assembly Elections of 1988

Name of Constituency	*District*	*Name of CPI Candidate*	*Votes Polled by CPI*	*Total Valid Votes Polled*	*Party that Won*
War-Jaintia	Jaintia Hills	Babyson Pakyntein	126	11,459	INC
Mawhati	Ri-bhoi	Orister Syngkli	25	9,643	HPU
Nongspung	East Khasi Hills	Fasterwell Marbaniang	257	11,517	HSPDP
Pynthorumkhrah	East Khasi Hills	Dalington Dympep	185	9,473	Independent
Laban	East Khasi Hills	Jokendro Lanong	252	7,830	HPU
Nongstoin	West Khasi Hills	Rosterwell Thabah	47	12,934	HSPDP
Phulbari	West Garo Hills	Nripendra Mishra	170	12,871	HPU
Dalu	West Garo Hills	Robin Rema	840	7,964	INC
Mahendraganj	West Garo Hills	Alauddin Sheik	304	10,177	HPU

Source: Meghalaya Election Handbook, February, 1988.

Table 8: CPI and State Assembly Elections of 1993

Name of Constituency	*District*	*Name of CPI Candidate*	*Votes Polled by CPI*	*Total Valid Votes Polled*	*Party that Won*
Nongspung	East Khasi Hills	Fasterwell Marbaniang	757	15,346	HSPDP
Pynthorum-khrah	East Khasi Hills	Bimolendu K. Deb Roy	114	14,153	INC
Phulbari	West Garo Hills	Lutfur Pradhani	161	15,635	Independent
Mahendra-ganj	West Garo Hills	Alauddin Sheik	106	12,418	MPPP

Source: Meghalaya Election Handbook, February, 1993.

Table 9. CPI and State Assembly Elections of 1998

Name of Constituency	*District*	*Name of CPI Candidate*	*Votes Polled by CPI*	*Total Valid Votes Polled*	*Party that Won*
Mawhati	Ri-bhoi	Marius Nongrum	143	13,877	INC
Jirang	Ri-bhoi	Marshal Wahlang	220	13,596	INC
Nongspung	East Khasi Hills	Jied Kharbteng	211	16,016	UDP
Sohiong	East Khasi Hills	Insee Allthings Marbaniang	180	17.900	UDP

Laban	East Khasi Hills	Fasterwell Marbaniang	98	8,500	BJP
Mawsynram	East Khasi Hills	Domison Marak	200	12,551	UDP
Mawkyrwat	West Khasi Hills	Nimton Lyngdoh	99	14,110	UDP
Phulbari	West Garo Hills	Md. Lutfor Prodhani	157	17,439	Independent
Mahendraganj	West Garo Hills	Alauddin Sheik	79	13,357	INC

Source: Meghalaya Election Handbook, February, 1998.

Table 10. CPI and State Assembly Elections of 2003

Name of Constituency	*District*	*Name of CPI Candidate*	*Votes Polled by CPI*	*Total Valid Votes Polled*	*Party that Won*
Mawkyrwat	West Khasi Hills	Khrawbok Mawliem	74	15,695	UDP
Dadenggiri	West Garo Hills	Witherson Marak	250	18,371	NCP
Ampatigiri	West Garo Hills	Ruparth Areng	227	17,271	INC

Source: Assembly Elections 2003 (Meghalaya) - Statistical Report.

Table 11. Percentage of votes secured by CPI in the State Assembly Elections of 1988, 1993, 1998 and 2003

Year	*No. of Candidates fielded by CPI*	*Percentage of votes polled by CPI*
1988	9	0.27%
1993	4	1.9% (approximately)
1998	9	1.08% (approximately)
2003	3	1.07% (approximately)

Source: Meghalaya Election Handbooks of 1988,1993 and 1998 and Assembly Elections 2003 - Statistical Report.

An analysis of the tables prepared above reveals the following :

First, the CPI contested all the Assembly Elections held so far in Meghalaya, presumably to register its presence, in spite of recurrent failures in electoral politics of the State. It may be argued, however, that mere participation of CPI in electoral politics without any taste of success for thirty years has raised a big question mark over the future prospects of radical politics in Meghalaya. As a matter of fact, the party's support-base seems to have dwindled with every successive election. Although there was a marginal increase in its share of votes in 1993, this was followed by a decline in 1998 and 2003. The above tables demonstrate that the CPI's share in total votes polled is meagre.

Secondly, a glance at the constituencies from which the CPI contested elections shows that the party has been consistently putting up candidates from West Garo Hills district. This implies that the

CPI has been able to build up a kind of support-structure in that district, although it failed to translate that support into concrete votes. It may be noted in this connection that A. Sheik who contested from Mahendraganj in the three consecutive elections on CPI ticket, polled 304,106 and 79 votes respectively in 1988, 1993 and 1998. Such a decline in individual vote share is actually reflective of an overall decline in the CPI's vote share. As far as the party's electoral potential in other districts is concerned, it may be observed that its base in Ri-Bhoi is extremely fragile except for a negligible presence in Mawhati. The party's position is more or less similar in West Khasi Hills, barring a token presence in Mawkyrwat. The CPI does not seem to have any base in Jaintia Hills. It appears that in East Khasi Hills, the CPI has been testing its fortune from a number of constituencies till 1998, but finally gave up this strategy in 2003 when no candidates were set up from the district. It may be noted here that the CPI kept on shifting from one constituency to the other instead of sticking to specific constituencies and nurturing them and this seems to be a major drawback in its poll strategy. For instance, the party contested three consecutive elections from Phulbari and Mahendraganj in West Garo Hills till 1998, but decided to shift to Ampatigiri and Dadenggiri in 2003. This does not seem to be a sound proposition because the CPI was unlikely to come up with any solid organizational base to back its candidates in two new constituencies within a short period.

Thirdly, it appears that the CPI contested mostly from the rural constituencies. The party set up candidates occasionally from urban constituencies, but its failure was more pronounced in such constituencies and its candidates lost by a huge margin of votes. It is worthwhile to note that the CPI has created a record of sorts in the electoral politics of Meghalaya, with all its candidates forfeiting their security deposits in their respective constituencies in all the Assembly Elections held so far.

Fourthly, what intrigues an observer of electoral politics in Meghalaya is the fact that the CPI has lost ground to new political parties entering the electoral fray and even to independent candidates. Radical politics has not only been successfully counteracted by regional politics, but also by rightist elements in the political spectrum. The obvious reference here is to the phenomenal success of regional political parties on the one hand and a rise in the prospects of the Bharatiya Janata Party (BJP) on the other. Although the BJP is a relatively new entrant in the electoral politics of Meghalaya, it succeeded in constituencies like Laban and Pynthorumkhrah where the electorate comprises a substantial number of Christian voters, indicating the party's ability to dispel its pro-Hindu image among a mixed electorate. In contrast, this phenomenon highlights the CPI's failure to carry on effective propaganda to allay popular fears that the party is against religion.

It appears that during the last three decades of experience in electoral politics, the CPI has been disadvantaged by its inability to generate charismatic leadership who could have converted at least a section of the toiling masses into a solid vote bank for the party. In this context, it is striking to note that the CPI has also failed to throw up a credible woman leadership during the last thirty years of its existence in Meghalaya. As a consequence, the CPI could not field a single woman candidate in the Assembly Elections held so far in the state. This no doubt negates the CPI's claim to be a progressive and Democratic Party.

To sum up this discussion, it may be noted that the CPI's poll strategy is also marked by a failure to choose the right candidate for a particular constituency. For instance - In 1998, Mr. Domison Marak, a Garo, was fielded as the CPI candidate from Mawsynram, a predominantly Khasi Constituency. The move was bound to fail and Mr. Marak could gather only 200 out of 12,551 voted votes. Incidentally, Mr. S. N. Marak, an Independent Garo Candidate from the same constituency, was far ahead of the CPI nominee with 2239 votes, thereby implying that the bulk of votes from the Garo community was captured by the Independent candidate. While it may be argued that ethnic mobilization is not in conformity with the CPI's ideology, it appears that the party has also failed to mobilize voters on class basis. Finally, in 2003, the CPI seems to have made a more realistic assessment of its capabilities and prospects in electoral politics and this was reflected in its strategy of fielding less number of candidates in the Assembly Elections of Meghalaya, in sharp contrast to previous elections.

A discussion on the CPI's views regarding the "Problem of Influx" in Meghalaya may help us in our analysis of the CPI's electoral setbacks. The communists declare in categorical terms that no foreigner can stay in any part of the country illegally and call for the detection and deportation of foreigners in accordance with the law of the land.[55] At the same time, the Communists are strongly opposed to the dubbing of everybody belonging to a particular ethnic or linguistic group as a foreigner. The CPI recapitulates that after the annexation of the hills by the British and the establishment of the Administrative Headquarter in Shillong, many English educated Bengalis were employed in Government Service, some of whom settled here after retirement. While referring to the influx of Bengalis from erstwhile East Pakistan that followed the partition of the country, the CPI points out that the assurance of the Indian leadership to provide refuge to those who wanted to migrate to India should not amount to throwing open Indian territory to anybody and everybody and allowing Indians to be reduced to minorities in their own states. The CPI refers to the customary laws prevailing in Meghalaya which prevent the settlement of non-tribals on tribal land without the permission of headmen and therefore, rules out the possibility of occupation of land by refugees.[56]

The CPI traces the origin of the Nepali population in Meghalaya to the British period when Nepalis were recruited to the army and were encouraged to settle here. Some Nepalis accustomed to certain kinds of hard labour, grazing and milk trade were also allowed to settle by the local authorities. Later, the District Council issued trading licences to some Nepalis living in the rural areas and those who did not obtain the licence had to quit. In most of the offices of the State Government, Nepali Chowkidars or Peons may be found because these jobs were not preferred by others. Although there was no passport-visa system regulating travel between India and Nepal in the past, some restrictions have now been imposed by the Government of India.[57]

Quoting the Census Report of 1971, the CPI points out that the tribal population of Meghalaya was 80.49% of the total population, 1% was Scheduled Caste and the remaining 18.5% was the other non-tribal population. Following the creation of Meghalaya and the shifting of the capital of Assam from Shillong to Gauhati, a large number of non-tribal populations also shifted there. Apprehending a sudden depression of the economy, the Government of Meghalaya approached the Centre which in turn, shifted some of its regional offices to Shillong. But since most of the non-tribal employees serving in these offices hold transferable posts, the question of their settling here permanently does not arise.[58]

The CPI, however, does not rule out the possibility of the staying back of a number of refugees from erstwhile East Pakistan who came to Meghalaya in the wake of the liberation war. The CPI cites official records to point out that during December, 1971 - January 1980, 8,829 Bangladesh nationals were detected in Meghalaya of whom 7,358 were deported without prosecution and 1,349 were deported after prosecution. As regards the allegations of a phenomenal increase in the number of non-tribal voters in the electoral roll of the state and attempts to link it to the influx of foreigners, the CPI refers to the statement of the Chief Minister in the State Assembly on March 19, 1980, declaring that the total non-tribal voters in the Shillong Parliamentary Constituency was 9.9% of the total voters in 1978 and 9.21% in 1979 while the same in Tura Parliamentary Constituency in 1978 was 12.9% and in 1979, it was 13.25% of the total voters. The CPI feels that these figures do not show any phenomenal increase in the percentage of non-tribal voters and hence the fear of being outnumbered by non-tribals and "foreigners" was unfounded.[59]

As to the question raised about the possibility of an increase in the number of non-tribal members of the Assembly, the CPI points out that a slight redelimitation of the Assembly constituencies can make it impossible for any non-tribal candidate as such to get elected unless a political party with a base among the tribal population would back a non-tribal candidate. In the existing constituencies also, if the voting is not guided by political choice, but according to tribal and non-tribal basis, with a single tribal candidate in the field, even these 7 members could not have been elected. It does not seem likely to the CPI that 7 members can so influence the remaining 53 members as to change the policy of the State Government in the interest of the non-tribals to the detriment of the interest of the tribal people of Meghalaya.[60]

While the CPI feels the need for vigilance against being swamped by non-tribals, it refers to the difficulties of finding any accommodation in Meghalaya because of strict restrictions on purchase of land by a non-tribal and on business operations, the latter being regulated by the issuing of trading licence by the District Councils. The CPI calls for due respect to the rights and privileges of minorities living in Meghalaya in return for the respect of tribal aspirations displayed by the majority communities. The CPI reminds the people of Meghalaya that their perspective should not be to remain tribal for ever, but to develop rapidly in order to catch up with the rest of the country in search of a better future, without of course, giving up their distinct cultural identity. The CPI concludes by emphasizing the need of greater vigilance across the international border to check illegal infiltration and seeks to strengthen its attitude of solidarity with tribal aspirations by recalling that it was the first of the national parties to support the demand for Meghalaya as a separate state.[61]

Honestly speaking, the CPI's views on the problem of influx seems to characterize it as a pro-minority party. Though the CPI maintains that it does not neglect the rights of tribals, its detailed analysis more or less nullifying the possibilities of the tribal population being swamped by non-tribals may not have convinced the majority of the tribals. While the CPI may have been very sincere in its suggestion of transcending beyond the label of being a 'tribal', this may not have been received favourably by the tribal masses and may have made them suspicious of the CPI's intentions. Thus, the CPI's views on this sensitive issue which is considered to be of vital importance for the survival of the tribal communities in Meghalaya might have acted against its prospects of capturing a substantial number of tribal votes.

We may summarize the factors responsible for the CPI's electoral setbacks in Meghalaya as follows:

First of all, there appears to be a fear psychosis among the tribal population of Meghalaya that communists do not allow people to worship God and practice religion in their own ways. Dalington Dympep and Robin Rema who themselves contested elections as CPI nominees are strongly of the opinion that characterization of the communists as anti-religious through propaganda carried on by ecclesiastical organizations had a profound impact on the choice of voters of various constituencies which acted against the electoral prospects of the CPI.[62] As S. Sahay observed, "Religions and rituals are in the Indian Psyche and the best one can hope for is reform, not abandonment. Even the Marxists have found themselves constricted by religion and castes in the country and fielded candidates to suit their electoral prospects more than their ideologies".[63] The CPI declares without any reservation that it respects people's faith and their right to worship God and practise religion according to their own choice and that it stands for absolute religious freedom, its belief being that the State should be above all religions and it must not interfere with people's freedom of religion.[64] However, the CPI's failure in the electoral politics of Meghalaya cannot be attributed to the religious factor alone. Even if religion does play a role unfavourable for the CPI, there can be no doubt that the CPI has failed miserably to carry on counter-propaganda to challenge the allegations levelled against it.

Another factor responsible for the CPI's debacle in various elections is the inadequacy of funds at the party's disposal. The CPI can spend only a few thousand rupees for each candidate fielded by it as against several lakhs spent by other dominant parties. The party cannot even afford a car and therefore its campaigning at the time of elections is extremely limited.[65] Money plays an important role during all elections in Meghalaya as in other parts of the country. In the electoral battle, the CPI turns out to be an unequal competitor, unable to match the resources at the command of other parties.

A look at the CPI's membership since pre-Independence days shows that the history of the CPI in the hill areas of Assam is marked by the absence of tribal leaders. Because of its failure to recruit tribal cadres, the CPI continued to be identified as a party of local Bengalis. In an area dominated by tribals, the CPI was perhaps viewed as an organization based on Bengali values. The CPI in Meghalaya turns to West Bengal for major policy guidelines and most of the party literature received from West Bengal are published in Bengali. In a tribal area, the failure to establish rapport with the tribals is a major handicap for the growth of the CPI. Recently, of course, the CPI seems to have succeeded somewhat in dispelling such misgivings as a result of which some tribals have been enrolled as members of the CPI. A number of tribal youth have now started associating themselves with the party's activities. However, some misgivings about the communists still remain and the tribal voters in general are still not prepared to vote for the CPI. On the other hand, the non-tribals do not seem to be convinced of the CPI's ability to protect the interests of the minorities. Thus, the CPI finds itself in a peculiar situation in which it cannot rely on the support of either tribal or non-tribal voters.

The CPI's views on the issue of foreign nationals reflect a kind of pro-minority bias. Moreover, the CPI's attempt to look at the interests of the tribals at par with those of non-tribals seems to have hurt the sentiments of the former, without generating greater confidence in the latter.

P.C. Biswas observes that as the electorate in Meghalaya was not politically educated, the voters were not in a position to judge the parties and the candidates set up by them on the basis of any programme or activity and hence the result of the election did not reflect the considered opinion of the voters and their political preferences.[66] The CPI may have made extraordinary promises in its election manifestoes, but according to Biswas, lack of political consciousness seems to have left the voters unmoved and unimpressed by them. This argument, however, does not carry much weight in view of the fact that an educated elite has come up in Meghalaya which is politically conscious and constitutes a significant section of the electorate. Therefore, lack of political consciousness among voters cannot be counted as a major factor responsible for poor electoral response for the CPI.

A few other factors seems to have contributed to the CPI's failure to achieve a significant breakthrough in the political life of Meghalaya.

During British rule, the Khasi, Jaintia and Garo Hills were among the Excluded Areas. Being thus separated from the national mainstream, these closed societies were under the strong influence of Christian missionaries. Later, when these areas were exposed to the rest of the country after Independence, the Congress was able to command considerable influence by virtue of its money power and power to grant permits, contracts, licence and provide other facilities. The CPI could build up its support-base only among those who were convinced by the communist ideology. In particular, the party's failure to draw the educated elite under its banner hampered the CPI's growth in Meghalaya on a mass scale.[67] The educated elite being an articulate group could have succeeded in popularizing and spreading the party's views and policies among various sections of the masses. But unfortunately for the CPI, it could not utilize the services of the intelligentsia for the spread of communist ideology in Meghalaya.

In Meghalaya, class relations have not yet been able to replace the clan relations. In the absence of industrialization, the proletariat also has not emerged. Thus, communist ideology has not found a fertile ground to operate in Meghalaya. The Communist Party has also failed to muster the support of the newly emerging educated elite in

Meghalaya because the CPI cannot be relied on to fulfill the aspirations of this class.

It seems that the CPI is trying to find scapegoats for its failures in the electoral politics of Meghalaya. Thus, members of the CPI cite the setting up of a large number of candidates in some constituencies as well as division of votes as responsible for the CPI's defeat in those constituencies. But in reality, the CPI does not appear to have strong organizations in Meghalaya to propagate its ideas among the masses and build up a safe and secure support-base. With increasing class polarization only, the communist ideology may become more relevant in the Meghalayan context and the CPI may look forward to a better future.

References

1. Author's discussions with Binoy Lahiri on 23rd December, 1987, in Shillong.
2. *Election Manifesto of Meghalaya Coordination Committee, Communist Party of India (1972),* Shillong, pp. 1-2.
3. *Ibid.,* pp. 2-4.
4. *Loc. cit.*
5. *Meghalaya Election Handbook, 1972,* pp. ii-iii.
6. *Ibid.,* p. 7.
7. *Ibid.,* p. 27.
8. *CPI Appeal to Voters,* Published by P. Misra for Meghalaya State Council, CPI, February 2, 1978, p. 2.

9. *Loc. cit.*
10. *Loc.cit.*
11. *Ibid.*, p. 3.
12. *Ibid,* pp. 3-4.
13. *Ibid.*, p. 4.
14. *CPI Appeal to Voters,* published by P. Misra on behalf of Meghalaya State Council, CPI, 1983, p. 2.
15. *Ibid.*, pp. 2-3.
16. *Ibid.*, pp. 3-4.
17. *Ibid.*, pp. 4-6.
18. *Meghalaya Election Handbook, February, 1983,* pp. 58, 69, 70, 79, 87 and 89. Actual Statistics on the margin by which the CPI candidates lost in the 1983 Assembly Election, were compiled by the author after deduction of votes secured by the CPI nominee from those secured by the elected candidate.
19. The information regarding the areas covered by Malki constituency as well as its population structure was obtained through a discussion with Binoy Lahiri on 3rd April, 1988, in Shillong. This information on areas covered by Malki could not be procured from any election documents because of the non-availability of old records.
20. *Ibid.*
21. Author's discussions with Robin Rema on 25th March, 1988, in Shillong.
22. *Ibid.*
23. P.C. Biswas, "Electoral Politics in North-East India with special reference to Meghalaya", in P.S. Dutta

(ed.), *Electoral Politics in North-East India,* (New Delhi, 1986), pp. 78-79.

24. *Ibid.,* p. 79.
25. *Election Commission (India) Order,* dated the 3rd February, 1978.
26. Author's discussions with Binoy Lahiri on 3rd April, 1988, in Shillong.
27. *Meghalaya Election Handbook,* February 1978, p. 39.
28. *Election Commission (India) Order,* dated the 3rd February, 1978.
29. Author's discussions with Dalington Dympep on 25th March, 1988, in Shillong.
30. *Election Commission (India) Order,* dated the 3rd February, 1988.
31. Author's discussions with Dympep, *op.cit.*
32. *Election Commission (India) Order,* dated the 3rd February, 1988.
33. Author's discussions with Robin Rema, *op.cit.*
34. *CPI's Election Manifesto,* 1978.
35. Author's discussions with Robin Rema, *op.cit.*
36. P.C. Biswas, *op.cit.,* p. 80.
37. S. Bawri, 'Electoral Politics in Meghalaya during the 1983 (Assembly) Elections (A Case Study of Mawkhar Constituency)' in P. S. Dutta (ed.), *op.cit.,* p. 128.
38. *Ibid.*, pp. 131 -132 and 144.
39. *Ibid.,* p. 137.
40. Author's discussions with Dympep, *op.cit.*

41. *Election Commission of India Order,* dated 6.1.83
42. Author's discussions with Dympep, *op.cit.*
43. Election Commission of India Order, dated 6.1.83, *op.cit.*
44. Author's discussions with Dympep, *op.cit.*
45. Author's discussions with Binoy Lahiri, *op.cit.*
46. Election Commission of India Order, dated 6.1.83, *op.cit.*
47. Author's discussions with Robin Rema, *op.cit.*
48. Election Commission of India Order, dated 6.1.83, *op.cit.*
49. Author's discussions with Robin Rema, *op.cit.*
50. Election Commission of India Order, dated 6.1.83, *op.cit.*
51. Author's discussions with Robin Rema, *op.cit.*
52. Election Commission of India Order, dated 6.1.83, *op.cit.*
53. Author's discussions with Dympep, *op.cit.*
54. Author's discussions with Prafulla Misra on 6th May, 1988.
55. This account is based on a Resolution entitled *Problem of Influx* issued in the first week of December, 1979 by Meghalaya State Council of CPI, see Appendix No. 2.
56. *Ibid.*
57. *Ibid.*
58. *Ibid.*
59. *Ibid.*

60. *Ibid.*
61. *Ibid.*
62. Discussions with Dympep and Rema, *op.cit.*
63. S. Sahay, 'Where is the Indian by the Way'? in the *Statesman,* September 11, 1986, p. 8.
64. *Draft Programme of the Meghalaya Co-ordination Committee of the Communist Party of India,* p. 3.
65. Author's discussions with Binoy Lahiri on 23rd December, 1987.
66. P.C. Biswas, *op.cit.,* pp. 81-82.
67. Author's discussions with Binoy Lahiri on 21st September, 1987 in Shillong.

5

Conclusion

The Communist Party of India, it seems, was formed by some Indian nationalists, the Muhajirs, in Tashkent during 1920-21. Later, the leadership of the CPI decided to adopt December 26, 1925, i.e., the date of the Kanpur Communist Conference as the date of the formation of the party. As we have seen in Chapter I, the formal establishment of the State unit of the CPI in Assam was preceded by more than a decade of preparatory work. The October Revolution inspired a large number of Assamese intellectuals in the twenties and thirties. The Meerut Trial, too, had its impact on the students of Assam as on those in the rest of the country. From amongst the students and youth who were imprisoned or expelled from educational institutions under the Cunningham Circular of May, 1929, quite a few became the cadres of Terrorist movement and later, of Communist Movement. Pro-Communist students seemed to have been playing an important role in the politics of Assam. Participation of the Communists in the protest movement against war efforts of the British Government contributed in a big way to the growth of anti-imperialist student movement in general and Students' Federation in particular. As we have explained in Chapter I, the general progress of trade unionism under the banner of the CPI was slow because of its pro-war policy. The historic Digboi strike acted as a catalyst for the CPI's growth in Assam in the sense that disenchantment with the Congress leadership brought a large number of youth under the influence of the Communist ideology. The trade union movement under Communist leadership could gain some ground because of the failure of the Congress to make its influence felt in the trade union front strongly. The overall growth of Kisan Sabhas in Assam remained sluggish through the war years. In May 1943, the first open Congress of CPI held in Bombay paved the way for the formation of the Assam Provincial Organizing Committee of the CPI. The role played by the Communists in the struggle against the Cabinet Mission proposal of 1946 for grouping Assam and Bengal helped in mobilizing public opinion against the scheme. Through the activities of Indian People's Theatre Association, the CPI was able to make a breakthrough amongst the intellectuals in Assam. However, after 1947, a militant policy of violent insurrection and guerilla activity advocated by a group of extremists within the Communist Party thoroughly isolated it from the masses. The CPI's ambiguous role on the language issue in 1960 led to a setback for the party in Assam. Following the split in the Communist movement, some dissenters in Assam formed a separate party committee of CPI (M). But despite the split in the communist movement, the CPI gained in influence and organizational strength during this period.

The problems and prospects of CPI in Meghalaya can be understood only in the context of the experiences of the party in the then Khasi, Jaintia and Garo Hills districts of Assam.

Because of the deep religiosity of the hills people and the fierce opposition of the church towards communists, the latter's influence on the Christian hills students was neither stable nor deep. During the late thirties, several all-India leaders with leftist inclinations visited Shillong leading to the radicalization of the students in Shillong. Shillong Students' Federation was formed in 1938 and by the middle of 1943, the Shillong Local Committee of CPI was formed at the initiative of local Bengalis. However, this unit could not recruit tribal cadres excepting one or two during the war years, although the Students' Federation was able to establish rapport with the hill students in various colleges of Assam and Calcutta and played an important role in politicizing the students of the hills of Assam. The Shillong Unit of the CPI proposed autonomy for the Hills. Its role in organizing different categories of workers and employees of Shillong cannot be underestimated. It also played a leading role in organizing a number of strikes, food movement, Oil, Refinery Movement etc. and came out openly in assisting the Bangladesh liberation movement in 1971.

As we have noted in Chapter I, a unit of the Communist party was set up in Garo Hills in the early sixties which organized the first ever Kisan demonstration in Garo Hills in 1969 and also organized some trade unions. Late Padmalochan Sarkar along with Chandramohan Hajong and Raimohan Hajong made a valuable contribution to the formation of the Communist Party in South Khasi Hills.

As the inauguration of the Autonomous State of Meghalaya took place in 1970, the Meghalaya Co-ordination Committee of the CPI was formed to carry on the activities of the party in the new administrative and political order. The demand for the constitution of a separate state for all the hill areas of Assam was first voiced in a meeting of the members of the Executive Committees of the Autonomous District Councils of the different Hills of Assam held in Shillong on 16 June, 1954. The demand was reiterated in the Assam Hills Tribal Leaders' Conference held at Tura. The Memorandum presented to the States Reorganization Commission by the hill leaders pressing for a separate State was, however, rejected.

S.K. Chaube points out that the substance of the hill state movement was the hillman's desire for an equal status with the Assamese plains people. It may be argued in this context that creation of the hill state or transfer of political power from the Assamese elite to the Khasi, Jaintia or Garo elite could not be expected to change the lot of the poor tribal and in that sense, the demand for a new State could not have been the demand of the tribal masses. Moreover, Chaube seems to believe that the Assamese people and the Hillmen did not have equal status. But it is difficult to understand as to how an ordinary Assamese was better off than an ordinary Hillman. Actually, the desire for an equal status seems to reflect the frustration of the educated elite of the Hills vis-a-vis the Assamese elite.

The CPI tried to understand the issue guided by its own ideology. The CPI looked at the problem of the hills people as basically a problem of their regeneration. The party viewed the hills people's urges for self-expression with profound sympathy and felt the need for the fulfilment of such aspirations in the interest of the integrity of the nation. Thus, unlike the APHLC and the Congress, the CPI took into consideration the question of national integration as well.

The CPI felt that the accumulated discontent of the people of the Hills areas was largely the creation of the Congress regime which had never taken kindly to the ligitimate urges and aspirations of the Hills people and adopted policies which only aggravated mistrust and frustration in the hill areas. The CPI regretted that a policy of balanced development of both the Hills and the Plains of Assam pursued by the Congress Government might have strengthened the forces of integration, as we have seen in Chapter II.

The CPI regarded the various proposals of the Government such as the Scottish Pattern of Autonomy, and the Nehru Plan of Autonomy as superficial, unscientific propositions lacking any basic appraisal of the real nature of the problem. The creation of a federal structure, as envisaged by the Government of India would, according to the CPI, neither ensure the unity and integrity of the people of the Hills and the Plains of Assam nor would it guarantee any rapid development of the region. The CPI also felt that the proposed Federation would reduce the status of Assam as a State. The CPI also rejected the notion of a composite Hill State because in its view, individual problems of each Hill could not be lumped up. At the initial stage, the party could not take a clear stand on this issue.

The CPI suggested that each of the hills tribes should be granted separate statehood, leaving open the options for more than one hill peoples, to unite and constitute a single State. The CPI rejected the idea of an integrated Assam that could be achieved only by applying force on the recalcitrant people of the hills. The party stood for emotional integration of the hills and the plains and that alone, in its view, could guarantee peace, unity, stability and prosperity of the region in the long run. The CPI also approved the existence of a number of Autonomous regions within the State of Assam. The party did not even object to one or more of these units opting out of Assam. Thus, on the Hill State issue, the CPI gave priority to the broader questions of the rights of small nationalities and national integration instead of being guided by the compulsions of its immediate reality through support for the demands of the most vocal section of the people of the area which later became Meghalaya. In an atmosphere charged with emotions, the party's talk of unity among the people of the plains and the hills in fact, bred suspicion and misunderstanding in the minds of the tribal population in spite of the fact that the party supported the demand of Hill State. Although the party issued some contradictory statements on the issue, it must be kept in mind that the Shillong branch of the CPI was then a part of the Assam CPI.

When the State of Meghalaya was finally inaugurated by the Prime Minister on 21 January, 1972, the CPI was the first national party to welcome and support the formation of Meghalaya as a separate State. However, by relating the demand for statehood with the aspirations of the emerging tribal elite, we may observe that the CPI might have lost considerable political mileage by its failure to support the hill State demand unequivocally in the initial stages. The CPI's support for an integrated Assam with safeguards to the hills people was not likely to suit the requirements of the emerging tribal elite which was eager to share political power.

Since the mass organizations of the Communist Party are the main source of its political power, an attempt has been made to examine the working of these organizations in Meghalaya in order to make an assessment of the party's organizational strength. The most prominent among the mass organizations of the CPI in Meghalaya are - Students' Federation and Youth Federation, National Federation of Indian Women (Mahila Samiti) and units of All India Kisan Sabha and All India Trade Union Congress. Apart from these organizations which are directly affiliated to the CPI, there are the All India Peace and Solidarity Organization and Indo-Soviet Cultural Society where the Communists play an active role along with other political parties.

Meghalaya State Council of All India Students' Federation was formally organized in 1972. The growth of the Students' Federation has been closely linked with that of the Communist Party itself. Still in its formative stage, the Students' Federation has not been able to build strong organizations anywhere in Meghalaya as we have shown in Chapter III. The ethnic disturbances in Meghalaya led to a substantial erosion in the strength of the AISF. Although the Students' Federation is not particularly strong in Meghalaya, it seems to have taken up the job of mobilizing the students and youth of the entire region. The Youth Federation organized several youth festivals and since 1973, elected members from the State participated in the World Youth Festivals once in every three or five years. But there is not much scope for expansion of the Youth Federation in Meghalaya because membership is based on small ethnic groups like Hajongs. It is interesting to note that the student and the youth organizations of the CPI are relatively more active at the cultural level in urban areas than at the grass roots political level. There is hardly any significant political activity carried out by these organizations.

The unit of All India Trade Union Congress was organized in Meghalaya in 1972. Meghalaya Jute Mill Workers' Union, Khasi Hills Saw Mill Workers' Union, Meghalaya PWD Master Roll Workers' Union, Shillong Municipal Harijan Mazdoor Union, Kumora Limestone Mining Workers' Union and Meghalaya Plywood Workers' Union were affiliated with the AITUC. But the AITUC could not retain its control over most of these unions and today, only PWD Master Roll Workers' Union and Shillong Municipal Harijan Mazdoor Union are controlled by the AITUC in Meghalaya. The rest of the unions had to be dissolved after being trapped by the clever manoeuvres of the management and the INTUC established its control over these unions.

All India Kisan Sabha has no statewide organizations covering the whole of Meghalaya. A Kisan Sabha called the Farmers' Union, was formed during 1976-77 in the Bhoi area of North Khasi Hills which fought for some agricultural reforms as well as took up some general problems of the area. Its struggle in defence of the farmers' rights made it quite popular in the area, but at present, it is not very active. In Jaintia Hills and Garo Hills also, Kisan Sabha organizations have been formed which deal mostly with local problems. On the whole, however, the CPI dominated peasants' organizations have not been able to make much headway in Meghalaya.

Meghalaya State level Committee of Indo-Soviet Cultural Society was formed in 1973. The ISCUS being a very broad forum, all those who have faith in Indo-Soviet friendship are eligible for its membership. Thus, along with CPI, all other political parties in Meghalaya except People's Demand Implementation Convention and even non-partymen are involved in its activities. According to the Cultural Exchange Agreement signed between Indo-Soviet Cultural Society and Soviet India Friendship Society, several cultural delegations from Meghalaya visited the USSR. However, absence of Government approval due to strict rules and regulations regarding foreigners' entry in this area has so far prevented the Meghalaya State Committee of ISCUS from officially entertaining delegations from the USSR. Of course, a number of ministers, legislators and other prominent persons are associated with the activities of ISCUS, thus lending greater credibility to this organization where the CPI is active.

Meghalaya State Council of National Federation of Indian Women was formed in 1973. Under the NFIW leadership, various women's days were observed in Meghalaya. The Meghalaya unit of NFIW also conducted eleven schools for the eradication of adult women illiteracy in Meghalaya. At present, however, the organization is not so active as it was in the past.

Thus, in Meghalaya, none of the mass organizations of the CPI have been able to achieve significant breakthrough in mobilizing different sections of the masses. The trade union movement, in particular, has suffered major setbacks and a number of trade unions formerly affiliated to the AITUC have switched over to the INTUC. It may be observed, however, that Indo-Soviet Cultural Society which has earned more credibility and public attention in Meghalaya is a front in which a number of political parties other than the CPI are actively involved. It, therefore, appears that if the CPI adopts a flexible stand by not insisting on the ideological commitments of those who participate in the activities of its organizations dealing with the problems of students and youth, it may succeed in spreading its ideas among a larger section of the population which may, in turn, raise the level of consciousness paving the way for political mobilization on the communist lines.

In order to assess the impact of the Communist ideology on the political life of Meghalaya, we have examined the performance of the CPI in the Assembly Elections of 1972, 1978, 1983, 1988, 1993, 1998 and 2003. The CPI fielded two, four and seven candidates respectively in the first three elections, but all of its nominees were defeated and most of them forfeited their security deposits as well. In the 1972 election which was fought on the slogan of 'protection of tribal identity and protection of the tribal customs and traditions' and the slogan against the influx of foreigners, the CPI projected an economic programme and sought to support democratic political rights. However, its influence was too weak to have any impact on the electoral politics of Meghalaya. The electorate was left politically very backward and they did not go through any sort of mass movement on general popular issues like increase of prices, exploitation of local producers by the wholesale businessmen or any democratic issues and they could not demarcate the respective roles of different regional and the national parties from one another through their own experiences. During the 1978 General Election, a demand for 'quit outsiders' was accepted as the main election slogan of the regional parties. The CPI's stand on this particular issue was rather vague. While the party stood for defending the constitutional safeguards provided for the tribal people, the party found no contradiction between the legitimate rights of the tribal majority and the non-tribal minorities who were permanent inhabitants of the State. This position adopted by the CPI might have bred suspicion in the minds of the tribal voters who played safe by turning to the regional parties as the true protectors of their interests. In the General Election of 1972, the CPI polled 0.71% of total valid votes. In 1978, the party polled 0.97% of total valid votes and in 1983, it polled 0.65% of total valid votes. In the subsequent elections of 1988, 1993, 1998 and 2003, the CPI polled 0.27%, 1.9%, 1.08% and 1.07% of valid votes respectively. Thus, over the years, there has been a steady decline in the vote share of the CPI.

The CPI's failure in the electoral politics of Meghalaya cannot be attributed to the religious factor only, as claimed by the members of the party repeatedly. Another factor responsible for the CPI's debacle in various elections is the inadequacy of funds at the party's disposal. Money plays an important role during all elections in Meghalaya as in other parts of the country. In the electoral battle, the CPI turns out to be an unequal competitor, unable to match the resources at the command of other parties.

The CPI's views on the issue of foreign nationals reflect a kind of pro-minority bias. Though the CPI maintains that it does not neglect the rights of tribals, a detailed analysis of its pronouncements show that it does not appreciate the possibilities of the tribal population being swamped by non-tribals. This in fact, makes it possible for the tribal elite to charge the CPI of practising anti-tribal politics. Thus, the CPI's views on this sensitive issue which is considered to be of vital importance for the survival of the tribal communities in Meghalaya might have acted against its prospects of capturing a substantial number of tribals votes.

The CPI's failure to draw any significant section of the tribal educated elite under its banner hampered the CPI's growth in Meghalaya on a mass scale. The educated elite being an articulate group could have succeeded in popularizing and spreading the party's views and policies among various sections of the masses. The CPI, however, could not utilize the services of the intelligentsia for the spread of the communist ideology in Meghalaya.

It is important to note that class relations have not yet replaced the clan relations in Meghalaya and the classes associated with industrial societies have not emerged, as we have shown in Chapter IV. As a party of the working class, therefore, the CPI has not found a fertile ground to operate here. With increasing class polarization, the Communist ideology may become more relevant in the Meghalayan context and the time may be ripe for the growth of the CPI in Meghalaya. The emergence of an educated elite which has established its hegemony over the State may be regarded as an important social phenomenon that has taken place in Meghalaya. The Communist Party which champions the cause of the workers is not likely to fulfil the aspirations of these sections of the society and therefore, the Communist ideology may not impress them much.

Moreover, the leadership of the Communist Party which is dominated by non-tribals may be looked upon more or less as an organization guided by non-tribal values. As we have shown in Chapter IV, the CPI in Meghalaya turns to West Bengal for major policy guidelines and most of the party literature received from West Bengal are published in Bengali. In a tribal area, the failure to establish rapport with the tribals and enroll them as members is a major handicap for the growth of the CPI in Meghalaya which needs to be remedied.

Mr. Dalington Dympep, veteran leader of the CPI in Meghalaya, admitted to the author that of late, the party has not been very active in Meghalaya. Lack of activities demonstrate an absence of sustained effort to rejuvenate and reinvigorate the party. An overall sense of despair and passivity seems to have gripped the CPI in Meghalaya.

To conclude, a new perspective on the future prospects of CPI may be explored. It may be recalled that Marx considered ethnicity, nationalism etc. as elements of 'false consciousness'. In Meghalaya, however, ethnicity is an essential ingredient of the social and political ethos. Herein lies the fundamental paradox of Communist ideology vis-a-vis the Meghalayan Society. In a State where the Student and Youth have been mobilized on ethnic basis, the CPI's model of class mobilization has been rendered irrelevant. Nevertheless, the CPI may be able to carve out a political space for itself if it can exploit the newly emerging socio-economic scenario in the State in its favour. In this context, it may be noted that in Meghalaya, a rudimentary polarization of social forces (not exactly identical with class formation) is taking place. In other words, disparities between different strata of the tribal society are getting wider and more pronounced. While a section of the tribal society has been able to make the best use of the constitutional safeguards and benefits meant for Scheduled Tribes, living conditions of the bulk of the tribal population have not improved to any significant extent after the achievement of Statehood. Till the formation of Meghalaya, fear of perceived domination by the plains people haunted the tribal psyche. But under the present dispensation, such fears seem to be misplaced and a new form of exploitation has gripped the tribal society. The contours of conflict are getting sharper, with the more prosperous strata of the tribal society subjecting the less prosperous and more numerous strata to various forms of subordination. In view of this development, the myth of a homogeneous tribal society has exploded, opening up the possibilities of mobilization of the exploited tribal masses against fellow tribal exploiters. This new phenomenon in tribal society offers vast opportunities to the CPI to carry on meaningful propaganda to sensitize the masses about the more subtle forms of exploitation by their tribal brethren, thereby neutralizing the process of ethnic and clan mobilization in Meghalaya.

Appendix 1

CPI Memorandum to Chavan, published in *Shillong Observer*, Thursday, June 1, 1967.

On behalf of the Assam State Council, Communist Party of India, the following memorandum was placed before the Union Home Minister, Shri Y. V. Chavan, on May 20 last at Gauhati.

> The alien imperialist rulers of the country pursued a policy of keeping the tribal people of the hills of Assam economically, socially, culturally and politically dwarfed deliberately retarding the normal process of developments of these people. This was quite in keeping with the Imperialist Plan of perpetuating their exploitation and domination of our country.

With the dawn of Independence it was expected that the new Government that came into power would make a serious assessment of the various pressing problems of the tribal people and evolve a new policy that would meet the aspirations of these people; bring them closer with the mainstream of Indian life.

The Assam State Council of C.P.I., however, note with regret that the Congress Government, far from adopting a policy in the above-mentioned direction, pursued a policy which was hardly different from that of the alien rulers. Consequently, the 20-year long Congress rule has not been able to draw the masses of people of the Hills of Assam nearer to their counterpart in the plains of the State. Instead, it has created the present problems in these areas in a vain bid to find out a solution of these problems. Now the Government of India has offered the proposal for reorganization of the composite State into a Federation.

By pursuing a narrow, sectarian policy with a scarcely hidden domineering outlook, the Congress Government, during the last twenty years, far from helping the process of emotional integration, has only helped the forces of disintegration. Little care was taken to develop the State, both the Hills and the Plains, in order to put the entire State on an even footing economically, politically or culturally, ensuring full flowering of the human and natural resources available in the region.

> Had the Congress Government pursued a policy of balanced development of both the Hills and the Plains of the State with an accelerated pace, the forces of integration might have been strengthened and the present situation might have been averted.

Urge for Regeneration

In the opinion of the Assam State Council of the C.P.I., the problem of the Hills of Assam is one of growth and development emanating from an urge for regeneration. Along with the advance of literacy and education, there has grown an urge among the tribal people for a rapid development of their economy, enrichment of their language and culture and social life. Under the impact of the operation of money economy and the capitalist system that has penetrated into the tribal socio-economic life of the region, the tribal socio-economic structure has been corroded; but a new socio-economic structure that could meet the newly awakened aspirations of the tribal people have not emerged because of the essentially erroneous policy pursued by the Congress Government. Nonetheless, the tribal dialects have been maturing into languages, with a system of grammar, and the distinct tribes in their respective geographical regions have been emerging as small, but distinct nationalities. These emerging nationalities have developed an urge to grow as distinct entities in the family of nationalities of India. However, this genuine urge of these people is sought to be exploited by certain reactionary elements, both within and without the tribal societies for the purpose of disintegration and discupation. The Congress Government by their innumerable omissions and commissions has only further strengthened these forces of disintegration, resulting in the present situation.

Faced with this situation in the course of the last several years the government tried in vain to offer some solution to this problem, without any attempt to go deep into it and the result was the various proposals such as the Scottish pattern of Autonomy, Nehru Plan of Autonomy and the like. But all these superficial, unscientific propositions lacked any basic appraisal of the real nature of the problem and met with failure. The latest in these series is the Federation proposal of the Government of India.

Reject Federation

We, on behalf of the State Council of the C.P.I., categorically reject the idea of reorganization of the present State of Assam on the basis of a Super-structure of Federation proposed by the Union Government. This idea of reorganization, in our opinion, is not scientific and it offers no real, lasting solution of the problem of the region. This proposed Super-State over two or more states does not ensure the unity and integration of the people of the Hills and the Plains of the present State of Assam, nor does it guarantee any rapid development of the region. On the contrary, the uneven development of the region which has bred suspicion, distrust and prejudice and engendered conflicts will not be removed by this scheme and consequently, the forces of disintegration will find a suitable ground to operate here under the proposed scheme of reorganization of the State. Moreover, the proposed Federation will reduce the status of Assam as a State.

In view of the above, we are of the opinion that each of the Hill peoples, viz., the Mizos, the Garos, the Khasis etc. should be granted full autonomy within their respective distinct region, with the right to constitute them into Union Territory, if any one of them so desire, with clear provision to remain, out of their volition, within the State of Assam as Autonomous region.

Hill State No Solution

In view of the uneven socio-economic, linguistic and cultural development of the different Hills, their problems cannot be lumped up and hence formation of a composite Hill State comprising all these hills will also offer no lasting solution to their problem and instead, such a state will, in no distant future, face the same conflict as vitiate the present composite State of Assam. Hence, in our view, formation of a Hill State, comprising all these hills, is also no solution of the problem of the region.

When these Hills have been granted the Autonomy, as suggested above, if any one or more of these opt out of the State of Assam, there should be a coordinating body without any superseding power, for the purpose of executing certain common plans and projects, without imposing a superstructure of a federation. That, in our opinion, will meet the requirements of the region.

Way to Real Unity

C.P.I., however, feels that the best interest of both

the Hills and the Plains will be served by an integrated Assam. But we do not subscribe to the views of those who would try to achieve that integration even by applying force on the Hills. Such a policy of forced integration may sound heroic. But this is not only undemocratic, but is also damaging to the interest of the country as a whole.

We, however, believe that by removing the causes of mutual suspicion, distrust and prejudice that have been accumulating for all these years, the ground will be paved for genuine mutual cooperation, unity and emotional integration of both the Hills and the Plains of the region. Even if some Hills opt out of Assam today, if the above-mentioned suggestion is accepted and implemented, there will be genuine unity in the days to come, out of the needs and experience of real life and that unity will have a more lasting ground to stand.

That is why we would propose that the Federation idea should be dropped altogether and the solution of the problem should be attempted on the above-mentioned scientific basis.

Appendix 2

Issued by Meghalaya State Council of CPI in the First Week of December, 1979

PROBLEM OF INFLUX

In October, 1977, the Meghalaya Pradesh, Congress Committees in its political conference in Shillong, adopted a resolution which said that influx of outsiders was the major problem facing the State of Meghalaya. Since then the other regional political parties have also been saying that this influx of outsiders threatened the very existence of the tribal people of Meghalaya, their ethnic and cultural identity is in danger.

Following the ugly incidents of violence in October and November, 1979 in Shillong, the term "outsiders" have been changed to "Foreigners". It is now said that thousands of these "foreigners" have been pouring in every day, threatening the very existence of the tribal people. It is said that because of the influx of these foreigners the population composition of Meghalaya has changed to the detriment of the tribal people.

Who are the foreigners? What is their number in Meghalaya? How do they affect the identity of the tribal people of the State? These questions require a cool deliberation so that we may have a clear idea of the problem and work out some concrete steps for the solution of the problem.

We Communists do not want any foreigner to stay in our country illegally. We want that if there is any foreigner in any part of the country, staying illegally, he should be found out and deported in accordance with the law of the land.

This, however, should not lead to a witch-hunt and everybody who belongs to a particular ethnic or linguistic group cannot and should not be dubbed a foreigner, rousing passion and creating animosity between people of different ethnic and linguistic groups.

So, it is necessary to have a clear idea of who is a foreigner. In a recent publication, stated to be of Tribal Women's Welfare and Development Association it has been asked; how can we distinguish between a Bengali here from one coming from Bangladesh? If this line of thinking governs our approach to this question, even a Bengali from Calcutta will become a "foreigner".

Let us look back a little to our history and try to put the problem in its proper perspective. Like all ancient peoples of our early history, how we came here or how we came to be known as Khasis or Garos and the like remains shrouded in mystery since there is no recorded account of it. We have some legends; but these by themselves cannot be a dependable basis of history. So, let us not take that into account, not at least for the purpose of determining the question of foreigner.

Judging by what happened in most other parts of the world, including this country, one can say that in the hoary past also some belonging to other ethnic groups, particularly those from the neighbouring areas, did come to our hills and settled here and became absorbed in our society. Over this there is no controversy and hence, we need not dwell at length on this.

After the British occupation of these hills, the Administrative headquarter of the British territory in this part, that is the territory that the British occupied, covering both the Surma Valley and the Brahmaputra valley, was set up in Cherrapunjee and then it was shifted to Shillong, a little over one hundred years back. As the administrative headquarter was established here, together with the British officials, many non-tribal, Indians also came here in the service of then government. Among them were many Bengalis. English education spread in Bengal first and hence English educated people for running the administration were recruited from among the Bengalis. Some of them, after their life-long service, on retirement, settled here. Following that first generation of Bengalis, some others came for trade and other business and thus a non-tribal community grew here and among them, numerically the largest chunk was the Bengalis. Till the time of Independence a very small number of Khasis or

Garos joined the services and the major chunk of people in the administrative service, particularly in the lower rung, were Bengalis. Some Bengalis also set up retail business and some got contracts etc. In schools and colleges, as these grew up here, some Bengalis came as teachers and some others began to practice as lawyers and doctors and the like. The bulk of them were concentrated in Shillong, some in Tura and only a very small number went to the rural areas.

After Independence, with the partition of the country, because of religious persecution of the Hindu minorities in Pakistan, there were waves of influx of Bengalis from what was East Pakistan then and Punjabis, Sindhis and others from West Pakistan. They came to all the States that have had common border with the then East Pakistan and West Pakistan. Some Muslims from different parts of India also migrated to Pakistan, though their total number may be less than that of the Hindus coming to this country from Pakistan. This became the inevitable consequence of the way Independence came to our country, with partition of the great subcontinent that had been a single entity earlier that now became two Independent countries. It has to be seen that people who fought shoulder to shoulder with those in present-day India and fought for India's freedom suddenly became 'foreigners' since the areas where they lived now became a separate country because of an agreement between the leadership of our country and the British Imperialism. Thus, those who were as much Indian as we are till August, 1947 became 'foreigners' after that date. Considering the entire historical background, the long tradition of common struggle against the British rulers and the fact that the Eastern part of Bengal, as well as the Western part of the subcontinent, were made into a separate country by an agreement between the leaders of India and the British Imperialists, our national leadership gave a solemn assurance to those who now found themselves in a different country, particularly those who had opposed partition of the country and hence were likely to be treated as unwanted there, that the door of this country would always remain open to them if and when they would find it difficult to live there.

As an inevitable result of the very basic theory of "two nations" on which Pakistan was created, the non-Muslim minority there were often subjected to various kinds of persecutions and a large number of them had to come over to this side of the Border. Some of them came to Khasi-Jaintia and Garo Hills also. Some of them were not only allowed to come; but also rehabilitated in certain parts of the territory which is now our State of Meghalaya. This is a price that we have to pay for the partition of the country; this is the price that those who once had their own homeland, at least a humble home and hearth, just like our people and were now uprooted from there had to pay for the freedom of this country.

Shall we now consider them as "foreigners" and "invaders", will it be reasonable to say that we shall enjoy all the fruits of Independence and disown the inevitable liability coming with the Independence of the country?

Our people did not fail to realize this inevitable outcome of the partition of the country. They did accept this as inevitable.

However, this does not mean that we shall throw open our territory to just anybody who comes and allow ourselves to be reduced to a minority in our own State.

In realization of the imperative necessity of some special safeguards in order to protect our small tribal communities, with our underdeveloped economy, the democratic people of our country and in response to the democratic public opinion, the framers of the Constitution embodied the Sixth Schedule to the Constitution of the country for the hill tribes of the then Assam, including the Khasis, the Jaintias and the Garos. This gave us a protective cover. Moreover, according to our customary laws no non-tribal could settle on our land, except in certain parts of Shillong and certain areas of Garo Hills, without the permission of the Syiems or Sirdars or Dolois or the Nokmas. Under the Sixth Schedule to the Constitution this right vested in the District Councils.

That is why the refugees from the then East Pakistan could not occupy land at their convenience in our State. In other States where they took shelter they might have done.

Thus at the time of creation of Meghalaya as a full-fledged State we had a Bengali population - the descendants of the early settlers and the refugees from East Pakistan legally rehabilitated by our Government.

In addition to that we have a Nepali population. How did they come here? The British rulers recruited Nepalis to their army. In order to facilitate this recruitment some Nepalis were encouraged to settle here. And those who retired from the army also settled here at the end of their service. In addition to that some Nepalis who are accustomed to certain kinds of hard labour, grazing and milk trade, came and are allowed to settle by the Syiems and Nokmas or other local authorities. After the District Councils took over the right of giving or refusing permission for settlement in certain cases trading licences were issued to the Nepalis who lived in the rural areas. Some who did not obtain the licence had to quit. Then there are other Nepalis who are engaged in various kinds of jobs, many of them day labourers who have not had any permanent settlement. They live and die where they work. Many of them have never seen Nepal at all.

In most of the offices of even our State Government one finds a Nepali chowkidar or a peon. Why? Can we say that they grabbed these jobs by force? Is it not a fact that they were selected for these jobs, to which our people generally did not go, by the lawful authority?

It has to be noted that India's relation with Nepal has evolved in the course of history. There has not been any passport-visa system regulating travel between the two countries. So, some people from Nepal come to India, work here for sometime and then go back - some of them settle down here. The same is the case with Indians also. But lately it has been felt necessary to regulate the travelling between these two countries and the Government of India has imposed certain restrictions. Accordingly, Nepalis coming to India after 1974 have had to obtain what is known as restricted area entry permit. These facts of history cannot be ignored while dealing with this question.

In 1971, according to census, the tribal population in the areas now in Meghalaya, was 80.49 percent of the total population of the area; 1 percent was Scheduled Caste and the remaining 18.51 percent was the other non-tribal population. In other words the total non-tribal population in the areas now in Meghalaya, including the Scheduled Castes, was 19.51 percent.

In every State of India, and in fact, in almost every country of the world, there is a certain percentage of people from other States or other countries. This is no particular peculiarity of our state alone and all these non-tribal people were not only Bengalis and Nepalis there were and are other non-tribals like Marwaris, Punjabis, Biharis and people from South Indian States like Tamils; Telegus; Malayalis etc. who are often called Madrasis, and Assamese, Manipuris etc. No doubt among the non-tribal population the two biggest chunks are Bengalis and Nepalis.

After 1972, when Meghalaya was created into a full fledged State of the country, the capital of Assam was shifted from Shillong to Gauhati and with it a large number of non-tribal population, Assamese as well as Bengalis and some Nepalis too, shifted there. No authoritative figure of these people who left Shillong then is available. On a rough estimate, it is said; about 35 thousand people left Shillong then. Among them there is a percentage of people who are permanently settled in Shillong for a long time and hence, their families may have been left behind. A small number of them also sold out their houses here in Shillong and left permanently.

The Government of Meghalaya at that time apprehended that as a result of this sudden decline in the population of Shillong, the economy of the areas directly dependent on the Shillong market, would slump. In order to prevent a sudden depression in the economy, the State Government approached the Centre to shift some of their regional offices to Shillong. Accordingly, some offices like the Geological Survey of India, Deputy Controller of

Defence Accounts, Anthropological Survey of India, Botanical Survey of India etc. were brought to Shillong. As these offices came, there came a non-tribal population who are serving in these offices and their families also came. But it has to be noted that most of these employees hold transferable posts and hence, after a few years one batch of them will go and another batch will come. These people are not likely to settle here permanently. So, they cannot bring about any radical change in the population composition of our State. Moreover, as these offices came here, some of our tribal people, however small their number at present may be, are also getting appointments in these offices, whereas earlier none of our tribal people got any jobs in these offices. It can be safely guessed that with the passage of time the percentage of tribal employees in these offices will increase and to that extent the percentage of non-tribal employees in these offices will decline. As an example we may note the case of All India Radio, Shillong station. At the initial stage there was practically no tribal employee in this station; but now a substantial number of the employees are tribals.

In 1971 when the people of the erstwhile East Pakistan fought for liberation to create Bangladesh, about 8 lakhs refugees came to Meghalaya from that country. Most of them were kept in the border areas and after the birth of Bangladesh most of them went back. But the possibility of some of them staying back cannot be ruled out. Among those who sought refuge here during the Bangladesh liberation war there were several thousand Garos and some Khasis also. How many of these people stayed back? There is no authoritative figures about them and hence all kinds of speculations about their numbers are there. It is only the 1981 census that can show clearly the population composition of our State and if there has been any change in the population composition of our State.

Another aspect of the problem raised by many is the infiltration into the State of People from Bangladesh after 1971 when that country was born, particularly after 1975, following the military coup and murder of Sheikh Mujib. On this also the Government so far could not give any clear picture of how many people have thus illegally entered this State. However, it has been officially stated that during the period from December, 1971 till January, 1980 altogether 8829 Bangladesh nationals were detected in the State. Of them, 1,962 were detected in Khasi Hills, 5,828 in Garo Hills and 1,039 in Jaintia Hills. Out of them, 7,358 were deported without prosecution and 1,349 were deported after prosecution; 93 persons were forwarded to jail custody, one person escaped, 3 died in jail and 25 were acquitted. Cases against 19 persons were pending enquiry and cases against 68 persons were pending trial, while 6 persons were undergoing jail sentence.

On an earlier occasion the figures of infiltrators detected were given officially. According to that figure -

in 1974	-	2,101	were detected
in 1975	-	1,627	
in 1977	-	401	
in 1978	-	309	
in 1979 (Sept.)	-	127	

These figures given by the Government shows that the rate of infiltration from Bangladesh has been declining from year to year.

Some have alleged that there has been a phenomenal increase in the number of non-tribal voters in the electoral roll of the State and all these can be accounted for by a heavy influx of foreigners. But the Chief Minister told the State Assembly on March 19, 1980 that the total non-tribal voters in the Shillong Parliamentary constituency which covers Khasi and Jaintia Hills was 9.9 percent of the total voters in 1978 and 9.21 percent in 1979 while the non-tribal voters in Tura Parliamentary constituency in 1978 was 12.9 percent and in 1979 it was 13.25 percent.

These figures do not show any phenomenal increase in the percentage of non-tribal voters. And all the non-tribals are not Bengalis and Nepalis only.

However, in the recent publication of the Tribal Women's Welfare and Development Association certain figures of voters in some Assembly constituencies have been quoted to show that there has been an increase in the non-tribal voters in the State. But the overall picture as quoted by the Chief Minister, shows a different picture. One cannot draw a convincing conclusion from the figures of a few of the Assembly constituencies about the actual position in the State as a whole. It is also known that in the enumeration of the voters' list in 1978 many of those who had voted earlier upto 1977 Lok Sabha election were also eliminated, while many of them were again enumerated in 1979. This happened not only in the case of non-tribal voters, but also in the case of tribal voters.

The above is not a picture that should create an alarm among us that we are being outnumbered by the non-tribals and "foreigners" in no distant future.

A question has been raised about the increase in the number of non-tribal members of the Assembly. If the total non-tribal population is 19.51 percent, and if it is assumed that all the non-tribal voters vote for only non-tribal candidates, there could be more than 11 non-tribal MLAs (exactly 11.706). There are 7 non-tribal MLAs in our 60 member Assembly which again is not disproportionate to the actual non-tribal population of the State. But it is not unknown to the political parties that even with the existing voters' list, just a slight redelimitation of the Assembly constituencies can make it impossible for any non-tribal as such to get elected unless a political party with a base among the tribal population would back a non-tribal candidate. In the existing constituencies also, if the voting is not according to political choice but according to tribal and non-tribal basis, with a single tribal candidate in the field even these 7 members could not have been elected. It is also not unknown that in certain cases some of those who are now the loudest in the campaign against "foreigners" themselves backed some non-tribal candidates and got them elected to defeat their political rivals.

But the most fundamental question here is whether the non-tribals have acquired a position in our political set up that can play a decisive role in shaping the policy of the State; whether the non-tribals can determine the policy of the State Government. Can 7 members influence the remaining 53 members so as to mould the policy of the State Government to the detriment of the interest of the tribal people? It does not seem likely that 7 members can so influence the remaining 53 members as to change the policy of the State Government in the interest of the non-tribals, against the interest of the tribal people of Meghalaya.

Can we ignore it that those who have no other "home State" than Meghalaya, those who have been inseparably linked up with the life in Meghalaya, should not be denied the same rights and privileges as enjoyed by the majority of the people of the State simply because they are of different origin and speak different language. Nonetheless, considering the under-developed stage of our economy the Constitution of the country itself has given us certain special safeguards against any possible threat of unequal competition by people belonging to the relatively advanced State of economy. And we have been exercising these special safeguards. It is under these special provisions in the Constitution that our District Councils could regulate settlement of people from other parts of the country in our State and lately the State Government has by a legislation that got the assent of the President of the country banned any transfer of land to any non-tribal for any purpose in any part of the State, except in a small part of Shillong town. Could any non-tribal member prevent this legislation?

One may rightly argue that unless we are vigilant a day may come when more and more non-tribal people from other parts of the country, particularly from Bangladesh may pour in and swamp us.

This apprehension, expressed by many, has also to be considered in the context of the existing reality and the scope for a non-tribal to find any accommodation here.

Under the existing law of our State no non-tribal can get his name registered in the Employment Exchange unless he can produce a permanent residence certificate. So, even if a non-tribal, particularly a Bangladeshi get into the State illegally, he cannot even get his name registered in the Employment Exchange, not to speak of getting a job.

No non-tribal can purchase any land anywhere in the State and hence, there is not even a remote possibility of a new comer non-tribal, whether from other parts of India or from any neighbouring country, to get settled in land.

Our District Councils have the sole right of issuing a trading licence to a non-tribal and without that licence no non-tribal can even establish a shop or any other business in our State.

So, if some people from Bangladesh illegally enter our State, how will he live here? Assuming that he has got a relation here and he will find shelter with that relation, is it reasonably possible for him to find shelter with that relation for an indefinite period? Most of the non-tribal people, particularly the Bengalis, are in service. And everybody knows the condition of the service holders who have been always clamouring for more Dearness Allowance and rise in salary because they cannot make ends meet. Can these people entertain a relation for any length of time? Some well established businessmen may maintain some relation for some time, but surely not for all time to come.

Moreover, who are the people who can normally feel inclined to migrate permanently to India from Bangladesh? Muslims in general are not likely to come in large number to settle in our State. And the bulk of the populations of Bangladesh now are Muslims.

It has also to be noted that a Bengali cannot live in a village in our State by concealing his identity because his physical feature, as well as language is distinctly different from that of our people, apart from the fact that according to our social custom no outsider can live in a village without the permission of the village headman.

Some people may enter our State on their way to Assam where they may conceal their identity. But they are not likely to stay permanently in our State simply because they cannot find a reasonable means of livelihood here.

TRIPURA

Some people say that our State may become another Tripura where the tribal population has been reduced to a minority by the continued influx of refugees from across the border.

It should be noted that in Tripura even in the pre-Independence days when it was under the Maharaja, Bengali was the official language and the administration was manned almost entirely by non-tribals. Since the former Maharaja's zemindary was in the adjacent plain district (now known as Comilla district of Bangladesh), and that was the major source of his revenue, he recruited officials for the administration from the zemindary. The tribals there were neglected by the Maharaja so that there was no tribal to man the administration.

It was under the leadership of the Communist Party that the tribals fought for their rights and abolition of the Raja's rule. In the post-Independence period, the Congress, failing to make any dent among the tribal people, dubbed them all as Communists and hence, relied on non-tribals for their political power. So, they did not give any right to the tribal people there.

And above everything else, while the tribal people of the former Assam got the protective cover of Sixth Schedule to the Constitution under which we have the District Councils with right over our land, the Tripura tribals are not covered by the Sixth Schedule. It is only the Communists who fought for Sixth Schedule for the tribals of Tripura. But the Central Government looked upon this demand as a "Communist Conspiracy" and hence, did not accept this demand. That is why the tribals of Tripura could not preserve their dominant position in that State.

It is only when the Left Front Government was formed there after the last election that legislation was passed for creation of District Council. But the Morarji Desai Government did not agree to amend the Constitution to give Sixth Schedule to the tribals of Tripura and hence the Left Front Government had to make legislation for District Council under the Seventh Schedule.

This background should make it clear that the Tripura situation has nothing in common with us and hence there can never be any comparison between our State and Tripura. We have our District Councils, we have already banned all transfer of lands to non-tribals and the political power in our State is with the Tribals. So, we do not think that under the existing condition our State can become another Tripura.

We have got enough of legal and constitutional means at our disposal to keep our State free from any illegal infiltrants, even if some of them sometime sneak in. Yet, none can dispute the necessity of maintaining of vigilance.

1. But does the situation warrant the type of agitation that has been going on in our State since October 1979? Does this agitation serve our best interest?

Our is small community in this vast country. It is the democratic tradition of the people of this great country that has helped us to get our State so that we may develop rapidly, without being swamped by relatively advanced people.

If the majority communities of the country had not respected our aspirations, our rights and privileges, could our small communities get all the assistance that we get now? Meghalaya was created as a full fledged State though about 96 percent of the State's expenditure has to be borne by the Central Government that collects its revenues by taxing the people of the rest of the country. Is it not then imperative on us to show due respect to the rights and privileges of the minorities living in our State? If we fail to do so, what impression will be created about us in the rest of the country?

Nowadays many people talk of maintaining our tribal identity. This point also needs a careful consideration. The perspective before us is surely not to remain tribal, for all times to come. Our perspective is to develop rapidly so that we may catch up with the rest of the country and march forward to a better and brighter future for ourselves. This does not mean giving up our distinct cultural identity, nor does it mean blindly sticking to the age-old social and economic life. What is required is firm, determined efforts for rapid development of the economy. Our agriculture needs radical reforms, arrangements have had to be made for marketing of our agricultural produce, and indus .es based on the raw materials available in the State have to be set up to generate employment and improve the economic condition of our people. We Communists in our programme for Meghalaya suggested that our tribal youth should be given training for manning the industries so that there would be little need for bringing in more people from other parts of the country to run our industries and there would be little problem of influx of outsiders.

If the successive Government did not take any appreciable step in this direction, can we put the blame on the foreigners? Which foreigner is responsible for the heavy indebtedness of our peasants? Who is responsible for our failure to make drinking water available to the village areas of our State or failure to make minimum medical facilities available to our rural masses?

Let us remember that our country is ruled by the capitalists who are concerned with only their profit. The vast masses of toiling people throughout the country have been fighting for bringing about a radical change in our socio-economic condition. It is by fighting shoulder to shoulder with these fighting people of the country that we can also bring about a radical change in our condition. We have to zealously guard our own culture, we have to further enrich it; we have to be vigilant against any infiltration of foreigners in our State and at the same time we have to join the nationwide struggle for a better social order in which there is no exploited, where everyone is guaranteed the fruit of his toil and all the working people are bound together by a bond of fraternity. Let us move along that line and build a brighter and better future for ourselves.

2. We have already a special cell of the Government to deal with the illegal infiltrators from across the border. It is now admitted on all hands that there should be better vigilance along the international border. For this purpose there should be more check-posts at shorter distance from one another and the Government of India has already agreed to strengthen the border security. The State Government is also raising additional Home Guard to man the border check posts. With all these measures we should be able to keep a better check on possible infiltration from across the border.

And 3. It may be recalled that our party, CPI, was the first among the national parties, to support the demand for Meghalaya as a separate State and campaigned at the national level for support to this demand. Eventually other parties also supported it and thus, through a national consensus, our State was born.

Bibliography

Assam Administrative Report, 1938-39.

Assam Labour Enquiry Committee Report 1921-22, (Government of Assam, Arbuthnot Committee).

Assam Legislative Assembly Proceedings.

Assam Police Abstracts of Intelligence (1940-1945).

Assembly Elections 2003 - Statistical Report.

Basic Statistics, North Eastern Council.

Communist Party of India Memorandum to Y. V. Chavan on May 20, 1987.

Communist Party of India Resolutions.

Constitution of the Communist Party of India.

Discussions with prominent leaders of the CPI like Prafulla Misra, Ranjit Kar, Binoy Lahiri, Robin Rema, Dalington Dympep, Montu Chakravarty and Umapada Deb.

Draft Programme of the Meghalaya Coordination Committee of the Communist Party of India.

Election Manifestoes of the Communist Party of India.

Leaflets published by the Communist Party of India.

Meghalaya Election Handbook, March 1972 (Issued by the Chief Electoral Officer, Meghalaya).

Meghalaya Election Handbook, February 1978 (Issued by the Chief Electoral Officer, Meghalaya).

Meghalaya Election Handbook, February, 1983

Meghalaya Election Handbook, February, 1988

Meghalaya Election Handbook, February, 1993

Meghalaya Election Handbook, February 1998.

Meghalaya Socio-Economic Survey.

Meghalaya Statistical Handbook, 1984 (Issued by the Directorate of Economics, Statistics and Evaluation, Meghalaya, Shillong)

Memorandum submitted to the Prime Minister of India by the Assam Provincial Committee of the Communist Party of India, November 24, 1947.

Memorandum to the States Reorganization Commission submitted by the Hills People of the Autonomous Districts (of Assam), Shillong, 1954.

Memorandum to the Commission on the Hill Areas of Assam submitted by the All Party Hill Leaders' Conference.

Programme of the Communist Party of India as adopted by the Eighth Congress of the Communist Party of India.

Report (By M. N. Mukherjee) of the Committee of Enquiry into the Affairs at Digboi (25 November, 1939).

Report of the Commission on the Hill Areas of Assam, Delhi, 1966.

Report of the States Reorganization Commission, Delhi, 1955.

Resolutions passed at the Aizawl Conference of the Hill Leaders on October 26-28, 1955.

Shri B. B. Lyngdoh's notes for Discussion with the Prime Minister (Nehru), 28th August, 1955.

Sixth Schedule

The Communist International Documents, 1919-43, (London, 1956), Vol. II.

(A) Books

Abbi, B. L., *North-East Region: Problems and Prospects of Development,* Chandigarh, 1984.

Adhikari, G. (ed.), *Documents of the History of Communist Party of India,* Vol. I, (1917-1922), New Delhi, 1971.

Ahmad, Muzaffar, *The Communist Party of India - Years of Formation,* Calcutta, 1959.

Ahmad, Muzaffar, *The Communist Party of India and Its Formation Abroad,* Calcutta, 1962.

Bandopadhyaya, Jayantanuja, *Indian Nationalism Versus International Communism,* Calcutta, 1966.

Bareh, H., *Meghalaya,* Shillong, 1974.

Barpujari, H. K., *Political History of Assam 1940-1947* (Vol. Three), Gauhati, 1980.

Bhargava, G. S., *Leaders of the Left,* Bombay, 1951.

Bhattacharya, Ajay, *Nankar Vidroha,* Vol. I, Dacca, 1973.

Bora, Phani, *Nagas: The Real Story,* New Delhi, 1956.

Brockway, Fenner, *Inside the Left,* London, 1942.

Bryan, William Jennings and Buch *The Rise and Growth of Indian Militant Nationalism,* Baroda, 1940.

Chaube, Shibanikinkar, *Hill Politics in North-East India,* Calcutta, 1973

Chaudhury, J. N., *The Khasi Canvas* (A Cultural and Political History), Shillong, 1978.

Datta Ray, B. (ed.), *The Emergence and Role of Middle Class in North-East India,* New Delhi, 1983.

Das, R. K., *Labour Movement in India,* Berlin, 1923.

Desai, A. R., *Social Background of Indian Nationalism,* London, 1948.

Dev, Narendra, *Socialism and National Revolution,* Bombay, 1946.

Druhe, David N., *Soviet Russia and Indian Communism,* New York, 1959.

Dutt, Clemens., *Conspiracy Against the King,* London, 1930.

Dutta, P. N., *Impact of the West on Khasis and Jaintias (*A Survey of Political, Economic and Social Changes), New Delhi, 1982.

Dutta, R. Palme *India Today,* Calcutta, 1970.

Elwyn, Verrier, *Nagaland,* Shillong, 1961.

Ghosh, Ajoy, *Selected Speeches and Writings,* Delhi, 1962.

Goel, Sitaram, *Netaji and the CPI,* Calcutta, 1955.

Guha, Amalendu, *Planter Raj to Swaraj, Freedom Struggle and Electoral Politics in Assam 1826-1947,* New Delhi, 1977.

Gupta, D. C., *Indian National Movement,* New Delhi, 1970.

Gupta, Pramatha, *Tribal People in Liberation Struggle,* Calcutta, 1983.

Haithcox, John Patrick, *Communism and Nationalism in India: M. N. Roy and Comintern Policy 1920-1939,* Bombay, 1971.

Hutchinson, L. H., *Conspiracy at Meerut,* London, 1935.

Joshi, P. C., *The CPI - Its Policy and Work in the War of Liberation,* London, 1942.

.............., *The Indian Communist Party,* London, 1942.

.............., *Congress and Communists,* Bombay, 1944.

.... *Communist Reply to Congress Working Committee's Charges,* Bombay, 1945.

.... *For the Final Bid for Power - The Communist Plan Explained,* Bombay, 1946.

Kautsky, John H., *Moscow and the Communist Party of India,* New York, 1956.

.... (ed.), *Political Changes in Underdeveloped Countries: Nationalism and Communism,* New York, 1966.

Kaye, Sir Cecil, *Communist in India,* Delhi, 1926.

Kennedy, Malcolm D., *A Short History of Communism in* Asia, New York, 1957.

Krishnan, N. K., *Communist Party Exposes the Fifth Column,* Bombay, 1943.

Lichtheim, George, *Marxism: An Historical and Critical Study,* London, 1961.

Limaye, Madhu, *The CPI- Facts and Fiction,* Hyderabad, 1951.

Marx, Karl, *Articles on India,* Bombay, 1943.

Masani, M. R., *The Communist Party of India: A Short History,* London, 1954.

McCall, A. G., *Lushai Chrysalis,* London, 1949.

Ming, Wang, *The Revolutionary Movement in the Colonial Countries,* New York, 1935.

Mitra, B. and Chakravarty, P. (ed.), *Rebel India,* Calcutta, 1946.

Narayan, J. P., *Why Socialism ?* Benares, 1936.

................., *Socialist Unity and the Congress Socialist Party,* Bombay, 1941.

Nibedon, Nirmal, *North East India: The Ethnic Explosion,* New Delhi, 1981.

Nollau, Gunther, *International Communism and World Revolution,* London, 1956.

Overstreet, Gene D. and Windmiller, Marshal, *Communism in India,* Bombay, 1960.

Rai Chaudhury, Satyabrata, *Leftist Movements in India 1917-1947,* Calcutta, 1977.

Ram, Mohan, *Maoism in India,* New Delhi, 1971.

................., *Indian Communism: Split Within a Split,* New Delhi, 1969.

Rao, V. V., *A Century of Tribal Politics in North-East India 1874-1974,* New Delhi, 1976.

Rao, B. Shiva., *The Industrial Worker in India,* London, 1939.

Reid, R., *Years of Change in Bengal and Assam,* London, 1966.

Sarin, V. I. K., *India's North-East in Flames,* New Delhi, 1980.

Sen, Soumen, *Social and State Formation in Khasi and Jaintia Hills,* Delhi, 1985.

Sen Gupta, Susmita, *Regionalism in Meghalaya,* New Delhi, 2005.

Spratt, Philip, *Blowing up India,* Calcutta, 1955.

(B) Articles

Bardhan, A. B., "Nationality Question in India", *Party Life, 25* (5), May, 1989.

Bishnu Borah, "Asamat Communist Party Gathanar Smriti", *Rupali Jayanti Sonwaran,* 1969.

Jadu Saikia, "Mor Communist Howar Smriti" Bharatar Communist Party, Assam Rajya Parishad, *Rupali Jayanti Sonwaran,* 1969.

Jyotirmoy Nandy, "Mor Koifiyat", *Rupali Jayanti Sonwaran.*

Karat, Prakash, "Concept of Regional Autonomy and its Concrete Applications in India", *Marxism,* 11(2), April - June, 1993.

Nigam Aditya, "Hegemony and Counter-Hegemony: Understanding Indian Communism", *Economic and Political Weekly,* Vol. XXXI, No. 14, April 6, 1996.

Phani Bora, "Asamat Communist Partyr Pachish Bachar" in CPI, Assam State Council, *Silver Jubilee Souvenir,* 1969.

Roy, Ajit, "Nationalism and the National Question in India: A Marxist Approach", *Marxist Review,* 18(3), September, 1985.

... "National Relations in Soviet Union: Theory and Practice", *Economic and Political Weekly,* 29 (1 -2), 1-8 January, 1994.

Srikanth, H., "Nationality Question in India: A Critique of Traditional Indian Marxist Interpretations", *Teaching Politics,* 17 (3-4), 1991.

Tarun Sen Deka, "Asamar Biplabi Communist Sambandhe Esar", *Rupali Jayanti Sonwaran,* 1969.

Vanaik, Achin, "Is there a Nationality Question in India", *Economic and Political Weekly,* Vol. XXIII, No. 44, October 29, 1988.

Vijay, G., "Mass Movements and Marxist Method", *Economic and Political Weekly,* Vol. XXX, No. 44, November 4, 1995.

(c) Newspapers

(i) *Assam Tribune* (Gauhati)

(ii) *Janamat* (Gauhati)

(iii) *Patriot* (New Delhi)

(iv) *Shillong Observer* (Shillong)

(v) *The Shillong Times* (Shillong)

(vi) *The Statesman* (Calcutta)

(D) Journals

(i) *Economic and Political Weekly*

(ii) *Frontier*

(iii) *Journal of the North-East India Council for Social Science Research*

(iv) *Mainstream*

(v) *New Age*

(vi) *North-East Quarterly*

(vii) *North-Eastern Affairs*

(viii) *Peoples' War*

(ix) *Peoples' Age*

(x) *The Communist.*

Index

A

AISF Conference 1986, 1988, 100

AISF views on international/ national issues, 98-99

AITU and CPI (M) infiltration in, 112-113

AITUC, 191

AITUC achievement/ limitations, 114

AITUC affiliation with workers unions, 108-109

AITUC demands, 109

AITUC procession demand Sept 2005, 113

AIYF Meghalaya Formation, membership,executive, 104-105

Alibaba Imti Ao (Naga leader) agitation of Grouping Scheme on land occupation,as Secretary of Assam, 36, 47

All Assam Students Educational conference 1946, 47

All India Kisan Sabha (AIKS) Meghalaya, 114-18,191

All India Peace and Solidarity Organization, 123-24

All India Students Federation, 18,19

All India Students Federation -formation,joining CPI, 97,99

All India Trade Union Congress (AITUC) Meghalaya Unit, 106, 108

All India Trade Union Congress Conference (Gauhati) 1945, 25

All Party Hill Leaders Conference (APHLC) - Meetings,Delegation to PM 1960, 70-71

Allison George, 23

Anti War demonstrations by Gauhati students 1941, 20

AOC charter of demands to govt 1938,strike, 26

APHLC - difference in, 73

APHLC acceptance of Autonomous State Plan-impact, 86

APHLC Memo to PM,1961, 85

Arrests of CPI leaders under British, 16

Assam Chhatra Sanmilan 1939, 19, 21

Assam Communists First Conference 1943, 32

Assam Congress Samajtantri Dal, 18

Assam Congress Socialist Party, 18

Assam CPI formation, 15

Assam economic depression 1930's, 23

Assam Hills Tribal leaders Conference 1954, 66

Assam Oil Company (AOC) labour union, 25

Assam political awakening, 17

Assam Provincial Congress Committee (APCC) declaration of Assamese as state language, 69

Assam Provincial Kisan Sabha meeting at Thekergaon 1946, 29

Assam Provincial Organizing Committee of CPI - formation 1943 33

Assam Provincial Trade Union Congress 24

Assam Reorganization (Meghalaya)Bill 85

Assam State Council, Communist Party Memorandum to Home minister 1967 75

Assam Valley District Committee 1943 under Bengal Provincial Committee, problems 32

Assamese - Bengali Fratricidal riots 1960 41

Assamese as State language - declaration 69

Assamese Language Act 41

Assembly Elections Meghalaya - CPI Performance, 133

Autonomous Regions - CPI on, 83

Autonomous State Plan, 85-86

B

Baghmara Constituency, 146

Bangladesh Mukti Sangram Sahayak Samiti 48

Bangladeshi infiltration, 217

Bengal Provincial Committee 32

Bhattacharya Achint 34

Bhattacharya Gaurishankar 19

Bhattacharya Gaurishankar 40

Bhattacharya Gaurishankar as President of Students Federation 19

Bhattacharya Jagganath 16

Biswas Pranesh Chandra 19-20

Books on Marxism (Publishing of) 37

Bora Phani 40

Borah Bishnu on Meerut trial 17

C

Cabinet Mission proposal on land allotment 36

Chaliha as CM 68,69

Chaube-views on language issues 70

Chaube, S.K, on hill problem 63

Chavan, Y. V (Home Minister) - CPI Memorandum 1967, 201 - 206

Chinese aggression (attitude to) 1962 41

Chinese aggression Stand/ dilemma on by CPI 42

Christian Hill Students approach towards CPI 44

Christian missionaries influence areas, 177

Civil Disobedience Movement in Assam, 17

Civil Disobedience Movement of thirties 30

Cominform Journal Program outlined 39

Comintern's Peasant International, 114

Commission recommendation for APHLC demands, 74

Communist as anti religious, 174

Communist Front in India - grouping, 96

Communist groups statewise, 14

Communist International, 13

Communist Manifesto 37

Communist Party of India,formation,13 13

Communist split 42

Congress Socialist Party groups 18

Constituencies/candidates from Meghalaya elections, 146

Constitutions 22nd Amendment,1969, 85

CPI ban Lifting 21

CPI extension of activities 35

CPI (M) formation in Assam, 43

CPI affiliation to Communist International 14

CPI and Assam peasant movement 27

CPI anti party activities - disciplinary action 41,42

CPI banned 1934-42 20

CPI deviant tendencies 39

CPI elections performance/ manifesto -impact, 133, 146 -47

CPI electrol setbacks in Meghalaya -factors of, 173 - 78

CPI first Constitution, 14

CPI formation, 183

CPI in Assembly Elections 1972 - 2003, 194 - 95

CPI leaders trial, 16

CPI manifesto at Gauhati Conference, 15

CPI Mass Organisation Role of, 95-96,190

CPI memo to Cabinet Mission, 35

CPI Memorandum to Home minister 1967, 75-82

CPI new directive 1950, 39

CPI patriotic image restoration, 22

CPI performance Meghalaya elections 1972,78,83, 133-36,139-45, 148 -49

CPI performance Meghalaya elections 1988,98 & 2003, 162-69

CPI poll strategy, 168

CPI prominent Mass Organisations in Meghalaya, 95-96

CPI Resolution on Assam land settlement, 28

CPI support of war decision, 21

CPI view on foreigners influx, 169-73,176,207

Crown Colony - idea of, 64

Cultural Activities role in awakening political consciousness, 36

Cunningham Circular, 17

D

Dalu onstituency, 154

Dasgupta Amiya, 19

Defence of India Rules condemnation, 20

Digboi strike, 184

Digboi -Tinsukhia area as protected, 26

Digboi unrest, 25

Dutta Barin, 46

Dutta, Dr Bhupendranath 15

Dympep, Dalington (CPI), 197

E

East Pakistan refugees CPI on, 212

Eastern India Tribal Union (EITU) - formation,stance on language, 68 - 69

Economic depression of Assam 1930's 23

Election strategy by other parties in 1983, 158

Ethnic issues/identity Meghalaya, 102-103

F

Farmers Union, 116-17, 191

Federal Plan - opposition,reaction to,1967, 84

Food Movement in Shillong, 48

Foreign Nationals issue - CPI on, 195

G

G.O.I historic announcement on reorganisation of states,1967, 75

Gandhi, Indira visit 1966, 75

Gandhi Irwin Pact, 17

Gauhati Vyayam Sangha joining Communist league 31

General Elections 1952, 1962, 40

General Elections 1957, 68

General Elections 1967, 43

General Elections 1978,83 - slogan, 154

General Elections and CPI : 1972 - 2003 performance, 195

Germany Soviet Union War, 21

Girls students Committees, 20

Golaghat District Krishak Sanmilan 1939, 30

Goswami Sriman Prafulla, 18

Guha, Amelendu on Hill politics-rise of, 64-65

H

Hajong Communists struggle, 48

Halowa Sabhas, 30

Hill autonomy, 185

Hill Movement - Demands,problems, 186-89

Hill Movement- split in, 69

Hill people -politicizing of, 44

Hill State demand for and position taken by political parties, 63

Hill/Council Executive meet /- conference 1954, 65,68

Hillmen exposure to outside world, 65

Hindi as regional language of Assam, 67

Humayun Kabir, 19, 45

I

Immigrant problem in Assam, 28

INA officers Trial protests, 22

Indian Peoples Theatre Association (IPTA) Role,fund collection, 37, 184

Indo German Democratic Friendship Association, 124

Indo Soviet Cultural Society Meghalaya, delegation,aim,conference, 119-21, 192

Infiltration - Bangla figures, 218

Influx problem - CPI on, 207

Integrated Assam CPI on, 83, 188

International Communist Movement, 13,

INTUC, 113

Irawat Singh (Manipur), 34

J

Joint Conference of Assam,Surma Valley and Shillong Student Federation 1940, 45

Joint Conference of Students Federation Shillong 1940, 19

K

Kanpur Communist Conference, 15, 183

Kar,Ranjit on ethnic issues Meghalaya, 102-103

Khasi- Jaintia Hills District and Marxist ideas, 44

Khasi Middle Class, 88

Kisan Sabhas growth, 184

Kisan Sabhas in Assam, 29

Konger, Macdonald, 36

Kothari Commission recommendations, 99
Kumora Limestone Workers Unoion, 112

L

Laban Assembly Constituency, 157
Labour Supervisers illegal appropriation of money, 110
Lahiri, Binoy as candidate in elections, 150
Lahiri on 1983 election strategy employed, 158-159
Land Reform Commission Report, 117-18
Language disturbances, 41
Language issue, 69
Language issue and CPI, 184
Lanong, Jokendra, 156
Leftist Parties (spread of), 31
Line System to settle problems of immigrants in Assam, 28

M

Mahanta Dada, 19
Mahila Atma Raksha Samity formation, organizing, 33, 47
Malki Constituency, 147
Mass Organisations -role of, for women, 95-96, 124
Mass Organisations -role of CPI, achievement, 125-27
Mass Organizations - Prominent, 190
Mawkhen/Mawprem Constituencies, 146
McMohan line crossing - condemnation, 41,42
Meerut Conspiracy Case, 16
Meerut Trial, 183
Meghalaya as autonomous State, 186, 189
Meghalaya Coordination Committee - CPI formation, 95
Meghalaya formation/ Statehood - support to - impact, 86,95
Meghalaya Jute Mills Workers Union and AITUC, 111
Meghalaya Legislative Assembly Election 1978, 136
Meghalaya Plywood Workers Union and AITUC, 108-109
Meghalaya State Committee of CPI 50
Meghalaya State Council of AISF, 190
Meghalaya State Council of CPI Memorandum on problem of influx 1979, 207
Meghalaya State Council of National Federation of Indian Women (NIFW), 193
Mehta Committee, 84-85
Middle class-rise of in Assam, 64

Militant Kisan Sabhas, 23
Misra Bireschandra, 29
Misra Biresh, 21, 34,39
Misra, Bani Prasanna, 87

N

Naga National Council demands, 49
Naga Problem and CPI, 49
Nankars peasants(settlement with) 1945, 30
National Congress of Women, Executive Committee, 124
National Federation of Indian Women (NIFW), 193
National Federation of Indian Women, 124-25
Natun Asam Weekly, propaganda activities by, 37
Naya Duniya, 34
Nehru Plan for APHLC demands- opposition to, 73-74
Nehru Plan of autonomy, 188
Nehru visit to Shillong(1955), 67
Nepalis in Meghalaya - CPI on, 170
Nepalis Population in Meghalaya - CPI on, 213
Non tribal leadership, 197
Non tribal MLA's voting for by tribals, 219
Non tribal people infiltration of, 221 -23

O

October Revolution, 15, 183
Oil Refinery Movement, 48

P

Peasant Conferences, 114
Peasant unions, 23
Peasants and Communist ideology, 29
Peoples War (Germany-Soviet Union), 21
Peoples War Theory,Wrong implementation, 32 - 33
Political development in Assam hills, 43
Post war years and economic front, 22
Private property rulesin Assam -Settlement Rules, 27
Professions,employment of Meghalaya Middle Class, 88
Provincial Conference of CPI 1948 -Gauhati, 38
Pynthorumkhrah Constituency, 150

Q

Quit Outsiders slogan, 154, 159

R

R.C.P.I Provincial Conference - Gauhati, 40
Radical Institute /Progressive Union Role in drawing Assam students into Marxism, 31
Rafiq Ahmed's account of CPI formation, 13 -14

Railway workers -Dibrugarh organizations, 24

Ranadive B.T, 38

RCPI led Assam Provincial Students Federation, 21

Red Flag Railway Workers Union, 33

Regional Federation appointment of 1967, 75

Regional language question, 67,69

Rema Robin, 49, 160

Revolutionary Communist Party Of India (Peasant agitation Inclusion in), 31

Revolutionary Communist Party Of India, 20

Roy,Burman on Tribal Politics, 87

Russian Cultural troupe (Tadjik) visit, 122-23

Ryot Sabhas, 23,30

S

Saikia Jadu on Meerut trial, 16 -17

Saikia Jaidunath, 30,32

Salt Movements, 33

Sangma, Bharat (CPI candidate), 159

Sangma, Capt Williamson, 68-70, 146

Sarma Krishna Nath, 30

Scientific Socialism, 18

Scottish pattern of autonomy, 188

Scottish Plan of Nehru, 71-72

Selsella Constituency, 148

Seperate Hill state-plea for,1954, 65-66

Shillong Local Committeeof CPI formation, organizing of workers union, 46,47

Shillong Municipal Harijan Mazdoor Union, 110

Shillong Municipal Workers' Union, 45

Shillong political movements/ movements organized by 45, 48

Shillong Students Federation, 185

Shillong Unit of CPI Movements by, 185

Shillong unrest in workers 1937-38, 45

Shillongs Students Federation-Formation/Movements, 98-99

Soviet concept, 44

Stalin, J.V ideology, 35

States Reorganization Commission (SRC) on separate hill state demand, 67

Strikes in factories 1918-22, 24

Student Movement - growth of, 183

Students/Youth Federation, 97

Sub- Nationalism Theory - Bani Prasanna Misra on, 87

Surma Valley District Committee formation 1941, 34

Surma Valley Hindu -Muslim unity in class organisations, 30

Swell, G.G - Nehru meet, 73-74

T

Tagore Saumyendranath (Gauhati visit 1938), 31

Tagore Soumen, 45

Tarun Sangha formation, 17 - 18

Tashkent and formation of CPI, 13, 15

Technical education demand, 67

Tibet revolt, 42

Tinsukhia Mail Robberies,A35 18

Trade union activists, 47

Trade union movement, 22

Tribal identity - maintaining of, views, 226

Tribal population in Meghalaya, 214

Tribals- Politics among -views on, 87

Tripura situation - comparison with, 223 - 25

Trotskyites group, 38

Tura Constituency, 160

U

Umroi Constituency, 151

USSR Constitution impact on Khasis 44

V

Vigilance along international borders, 228

Wage Board Report - implementation by AITUC, 113

War Jaintia Assembly, 161

War Jaintia Constituency, 147

Women- Mass Organization for, 124

Y

Youth Federation, 190 - 91

Youth Festival Shillong 1978, 102